Easy Dutch Oven Cookbook

101 Everyday One-Pot Meal Recipes with 8 Ingredients or Less

Louise Davidson

ISBN: 9798577423926

Printed in the United States

www.thecookbookpublisher.com

CONTENTS

INTRODUCTION

The Dutch oven is a real workhorse. It's been around since the 1700s, and it's endured so long because you can make so many culinary wonders using just this sturdy, heavy pot. That's right—you need to use only one pot for the entire cooking process! That simplifies cooking and saves precious time, so it's no wonder that this centuries-old device is now a star of smart 21st-century cooking.

The Dutch oven is versatile, too: you can use it for stove-top cooking or you can pop it in the oven. It can make soups, stews, pasta, fried foods, baked goods, and desserts in very little time. It enables one-pot cooking by replacing multiple utensils such as stockpots, saucepans, roasting and sauté pans, and pasta pots.

The advantages of the Dutch oven are almost endless. It is designed for maximum retention and utilization of cooking heat, making it an ideal pot for uniform braising. It cooks food evenly by equal distribution of heat. Its unique design prevents moisture loss; by locking in moisture, it improves the flavor profile to make aromatic and delicious meals every time. Once you start using a Dutch oven, it will become a permanent fixture in your kitchen. Why would you want to put it away when it allows you to cook almost anything, anytime, in mere minutes?

Cooking with fewer ingredients is nothing new, but it's a smart choice that allows you to recreate the magic of complex and time-consuming cuisines with less effort by tossing the right mix of ingredients into your Dutch oven. When you have only a few ingredients to use, you can plan ahead and stuff your pantry in advance with those essential ingredients. When most of your ingredients are just sitting on the shelf waiting to be added, it makes cooking super smooth and easy.

Quick and easy Dutch oven meals use fresh, nutritious, and flavorful ingredients. After a hard day at work, you deserve a hearty and healthy meal to satisfy your hunger. This book is an exclusive cookbook for people who believe in simplifying cooking by using a smart combination of ingredients to produce healthy meals in one pot—and that without compromising on rich flavors. Explore a truly versatile collection of quick and easy Dutch oven meals for the whole family.

Also, keep in mind that all the recipes from this collection can easily be used for cooking in the great outdoors with a Dutch oven during a camping trip.

Please note that all the recipes in this collection have 8-ingredients or less. Lots have 5 ingredients. How easy is that? Naturally, I do not count salt and pepper, cooking fat (butter, oil, cooking spray, ghee, etc.), and water in the 8 or less ingredient needed to do each recipe.

GET TO KNOW
YOUR DUTCH OVEN!

Simply put, a Dutch oven is just a big heavy pot with a lid. It's made of cast iron and is usually lined with enamel. The lid is tight-fitting, which allows the pot to retain moisture, heat, and flavor. Sometimes Dutch ovens are also called camp pots or bean pots. So what's so special about it? Why are its owners professing their undying love for it?

Let us count the ways:

- **It's versatile**. Because you can use it on the stovetop and in the oven, you can cook in almost any way you want — boil, fry, broil, bake, stew — you name it. Outdoor Dutch ovens can be used on camping trips with coal or briquettes as fuel.

- **It's pretty**. Many models come in colorful designs that dress up the kitchen shelves and tables. It has a vintage look. Dishes can be brought straight to the table without the need for a serving dish.

- **It's durable**. Many of its owners have had them for decades and, except for some discoloration and minor chipping, their pots still work like new. Of course, its durability may depend on the material and the brand.

- **It's a workhorse**. It's a trusty kitchen friend and helper that can do a variety of jobs in large quantities and for long hours.

- **It's energy-efficient**. The thick walls made of cast iron and the tight-fitting lid help distribute heat evenly, and retain it even after the pot has been removed from the heat source.

- **It makes food more healthy and delicious**. The tight lid helps keep in the flavors and the steady heat makes the meat super tender. The enamel lining also prevents any undesirable reactions between acidic food and metal.

- **It makes cooking easy**. Because you can go straight from stovetop to oven, a lot of messy and time-wasting steps are eliminated from the cooking process.

- **It's great for camping trips**. The camp Dutch oven makes it possible to prepare delicious meals, desserts, and bread on camping trips or cookouts. In the Appendix, at the end of the book, you will find a section about cooking in the great outdoors with a Dutch oven.

How Dutch Ovens Became a Part of American Tradition

The Dutch oven is not exactly Dutch. Dutch ovens have actually been around for centuries, and similar pots have been used in Japan, South Africa, Russia, and many European countries. However, its design is based on the technology that was first developed in the Netherlands. The Dutch were quite advanced in their know-how on making cast-iron posts. Britain was one of the countries that imported pots from the Netherlands. It was in the later part of the 1600s that a man named Abraham Darby decided to see how the pots were made. He brought the technology back to Britain, patented his own process based on what he'd picked up from the Dutch, and opened his own line of "Dutch" ovens. From Britain, the Dutch ovens made their way to America.

Dutch ovens are very much a part of the American cooking tradition. Paul Revere himself is said to have designed the flat lid to hold coals, as well as being credited with the addition of the pot's legs. These pots were considered heirloom treasures by their owners and were bequeathed to deserving descendants. Even George Washington's mother, Mary Ball Washington, is said to have included her Dutch ovens in her will, leaving them to her grandchildren, in 1788. The great explorers of the uncharted American territory, Lewis and Clark, brought their Dutch ovens with them during their expeditions. Mormon pioneers in the 1800s also brought theirs when they settled in the American northwest. In the 19th through to the 20th century, explorers in the mountains and on chuck wagons all brought their handy and hardy Dutch ovens with them, as did the 49ers of California and soldiers in the Civil War.

Dutch ovens may not be as popular as they were hundreds of years ago, but their popularity has slowly risen. The trend was said to have started in the 1980s when Dutch oven cook-offs were started. In 1997, Utah made the Dutch oven its official cooking pot. Texas and Arkansas have also named it their state pot.

Buying a Dutch Oven

You will first have to decide on the type of oven you need.

Types of Dutch Ovens

Cast iron – This is what most people have in mind when they think of the Dutch oven. It keeps heat well and is so durable it lasts for decades. It can be very heavy and a burden to carry on outdoor trips. If the pot isn't lined with enamel, it may need to be seasoned to prevent rusting, and iron from leeching into the food. Nowadays, most cast-iron cookware has already been pre-seasoned by the manufacturer.

Aluminum – This doesn't rust and is lighter in weight than cast iron. It's easy to clean and doesn't need seasoning. Aluminum heats up faster than cast iron, but it's not as durable.

Camp or Outdoor – Just like the ones that the pioneers and explorers used, this pot has a flat lid and three legs, according to Paul Revere's specifications. Coals can be placed on the lid for baking. Additionally, the lid can also be used as a frying pan or grill.

Enameled – Is non-reactive with acidic ingredients and doesn't require seasoning. However, it isn't non-stick, it chips, and it doesn't hold flavors.

Things to check out before buying:

- For second-hand pots, make sure there are no rusty spots, cracks, or chips.
- The lid should not be too loose-fitting nor too tight and difficult to remove.

- The metal should be thick and of a consistent thickness. Check the sides as well as the bottom of the pan.
- The size would depend on how much food you usually cook, and maybe the space in your kitchen. A 6-quart pot is usually adequate and large enough to roast a whole chicken.
- Consider your budget. The more expensive ones can last for generations. The cheaper ones may not last as long, but they tend to function just as well as the expensive ones.
- Handles should be easy to grasp, even when you're wearing mittens.

Giving Your Dutch Oven Some TLC

It's important to give your Dutch oven some tender loving care or TLC. The number one thing for non-enameled cast iron Dutch ovens is to maintain its non-stick layer and prevent rusting. These are general guidelines; it's still best to read the manufacturer's specific instructions.

Cleaning

This will help maintain your Dutch oven's non-stick layer and protect it from rust.
1. Clean with soap and hot water only when it is brand new. Do not use soap for subsequent cleanings.
2. After cooking, be sure to clean the oven while it is still warm, so its "pores" will be open.
3. Remove pieces of food and wipe clean with a cloth.
4. Pour hot water into the Dutch oven. Scrub any stuck food with a non-metal scrubber (nylon or plastic).
5. Remember, don't use soap as this will destroy the non-stick surface.
6. Pour out the water, wipe, rinse, and dry.
7. For hard-to-remove food bits, use a paste of kosher salt and hot water. Scrub, rinse, and wipe clean.

Oiling

1. Heat up the oven to open its pores.
2. When the pot is warm to the touch (not hot), wipe with a small amount of vegetable or olive oil, just enough to form a thin coating over the pot's interior.
3. Do not store your Dutch oven with the lid tightly shut. Leave it open or place paper or foil between the rim and the lid, to let air circulate in the pot.

Seasoning

This step may not be needed as most Dutch ovens nowadays have already been pre-seasoned. You may need to season yours if you bought it second hand, or if you see some rusty spots. Here's how:

1. Clean the pot according to the instructions above.
2. Preheat the oven to 350°F.
3. Place the pot and lid in the oven, upside down.
4. Allow the pot to heat until the handles are almost unbearable to touch.
5. Take the pot and lid out of the oven.
6. With a paper towel, rub the pot and lid with a small amount of shortening, just to make a thin layer. Cooking spray, butter, and margarine are also suitable. Do not use too much.
7. Rub all surfaces, inside and outside the pot and lid.
8. Place a pan or cookie sheet in the lower rack of the oven to catch any run-off.
9. Put the pot and lid, upside down, in the oven again.
10. Leave to bake for an hour. (Expect a lot of smoke.)
11. Let the Dutch oven and lid remain in the oven until cool.
12. Remove from oven and wipe clean.

Okay, so now that you've got your Dutch oven and you know how to care for it, you're all set to use it. It's time to take your favorite pot and put it to work in the kitchen to produce quick and easy mouthwatering meals. Let's get started.

BREAKFAST

Breakfast Chicken Casserole

Serves 8 | Prep. time 10 minutes | Cooking time 25 minutes

Ingredients
¼ cup butter
12 eggs
1 quart whole milk
1½ teaspoons Italian herb blend
1 teaspoon salt
½ teaspoon pepper
8 slices bread, diced
2 chicken breasts, cooked and shredded
1 pound cheddar cheese, grated

Directions
1. Spread the butter evenly over the inside surface of the Dutch oven.
2. Heat the Dutch oven to 350°F (175°C).
3. Beat the eggs in a bowl. Add the milk, Italian herbs, salt, and pepper. Mix well.
4. Make a layer of bread in the Dutch oven. Cover it with the shredded chicken.
5. Pour on the egg mixture.
6. Cover the Dutch oven and cook for 20–25 minutes.
7. Add the cheese, cover again, and cook for 10–15 minutes more until the eggs are well cooked.
8. Serve warm.

Nutrition (per serving)
Calories 587, Fat 23 g, carbs 18 g,
Protein 33 g, sodium 1254 mg

Classic Bacon and Eggs

*Serves 8 | Prep. time 10–15 minutes |
Cooking time 25 minutes*

Ingredients
1 pound bacon strips, chopped
1¼ pounds hash brown potatoes, refrigerated
8 large eggs
½ cup half-and-half cream
½–1 teaspoon hot pepper sauce (optional)
2 cups cheddar-Monterey Jack cheese, shredded

Directions
1. Heat the Dutch oven over medium-high heat.
2. Add the bacon and cook until crisp. Drain over paper towels and set aside.
3. Keep 2 tablespoons of the drippings in the oven. Discard the remaining drippings.
4. Add the potatoes.
5. Whisk the eggs and cream in a bowl. Add the pepper sauce. Mix well.
6. Pour the mixture over the potatoes. Add the bacon and cheese on top.
7. Cover the Dutch oven and cook for 20–25 minutes until the eggs are cooked well.
8. Serve warm.

Nutrition (per serving)
Calories 393, Fat 25 g, carbs 17 g,
Protein 21 g, sodium 907 mg

Ham Cheese Omelet

Serves 1 | Prep. time 5 minutes | Cooking time 5–8 minutes

Ingredients
1 tablespoon butter
3 eggs
3 tablespoons water
⅛ teaspoon salt
⅛ teaspoon pepper
½ cup cooked ham, cubed
¼ cup Swiss cheese, shredded

Directions
1. Add the butter to the Dutch oven and melt it over medium-high heat.
2. Whisk the eggs in a bowl. Add the water, salt, and pepper. Mix well.
3. Add the mixture to the Dutch oven and make a thin layer.
4. Cook until the eggs are set, then stir without breaking the layer.
5. Add the ham on one side and add the cheese on top.
6. Fold the other side over the filling.
7. Serve warm.

Nutrition (per serving)
Calories 530, Fat 40 g, carbs 4 g,
Protein 39 g, sodium 1551 mg

Sausage-Hash Morning

Serves 6 | Prep. time 10–15 minutes |
Cooking time 25 minutes

Ingredients
2 tablespoons olive oil
½ pound cooked Spanish chorizo or cooked Andouille sausage, finely chopped
4 celery ribs, finely chopped
1 medium onion, finely chopped
4 cloves garlic, minced
½ teaspoon salt
¼ teaspoon pepper
4 cups (2–3 medium) sweet potatoes, finely chopped

Directions
1. Add the oil to the Dutch oven and heat it over medium-high heat.
2. Add the sausage and stir-cook until evenly browned.
3. Add the other ingredients and stir-cook.
4. Simmer over low heat for about 15–20 minutes until the potatoes are cooked well, stirring occasionally.
5. Serve warm.

Nutrition (per serving)
Calories 226, Fat 12 g, carbs 22 g,
Protein 9 g, sodium 602 mg

Breakfast Sausage Casserole

Serves 4 | Prep time 10 minutes | Cooking time 25 minutes

Ingredients
2 tablespoons olive oil
2 pounds pork breakfast sausage
Salt and pepper to taste
2 pounds hash brown potatoes
8 large eggs
¼ cup heavy cream
2 cups shredded mozzarella cheese

Directions
1. Preheat the oven to 350°F (180°C).
2. Warm the olive oil in the Dutch oven over medium heat.
3. Add the pork breakfast sausage, break it up with a wooden spoon, and cook for 5–7 minutes.
4. Remove from the Dutch oven and set aside.
5. Spread the hash browns evenly in the bottom of the Dutch oven. Season with salt and pepper.
6. Gently brown the potatoes and place the cooked sausage on top of them.
7. Whisk the eggs with a fork and spread them on top of the potatoes and sausages.
8. Sprinkle with grated cheese.
9. Cover and bake for 20–25 minutes.
10. Serve warm.

Nutrition (per serving)
Calories 1432, Fat 96.8 g, carbs 83.1 g,
Protein 59.7 g, sodium 2870 mg

Biscuits and Gravy

Serves 4 | Prep time 10 minutes | Cooking time 25 minutes

Ingredients
2 tablespoons olive oil
1 (16-ounce) can of refrigerated jumbo buttermilk biscuits
1 pound pork breakfast sausages
¼ cup flour
2¼ cups whole milk
Salt and pepper to taste

Directions
1. Preheat the Dutch oven to 350°F (180°C).
2. Grease it well with olive oil or butter.
3. Place the biscuits in the heated Dutch oven, cover, and bake for about 25 minutes.
4. Remove the biscuits and set aside.
5. Break up the breakfast sausage and cook for about 5 minutes, stirring frequently.
6. Stir in the flour, mix well, and pour in the milk.
7. Cook for about 5 minutes until a sauce forms. Season with salt and pepper.
8. Serve the sausage gravy over the warm biscuits.

Nutrition (per serving)
Calories 866, Fat 53.3 g, carbs 68.2 g,
Protein 30.3 g, sodium 2181 mg

Dutch Oven Tater Tot Casserole

Serves 4 | Prep time 10 minutes | Cooking time 30 minutes

Ingredients
2 tablespoons olive oil
1 small onion, diced
1 pound ground beef
Salt and pepper to taste
2 (10½-ounce) cans cream of mushroom soup
2 pounds frozen tater tots
2 cups grated cheddar cheese

Directions
1. Warm the olive oil in the Dutch oven over medium heat. Add the diced onion and ground beef.
2. Season with salt and pepper and cook for about 10 minutes.
3. Stir in the cream of mushroom soup.
4. Arrange the tater tots on top and bake uncovered for about 25 minutes at 350°F (180°C).
5. Sprinkle in the cheese and bake for another 5–7 minutes.

Nutrition (per serving)
Calories 671, Fat 43.1 g, carbs 18.3 g,
Protein 50.8 g, sodium 1040 mg

Mushroom Frittata

Serves 4 | Prep time 10 minutes | Cooking time 30 minutes

Ingredients
2 tablespoons olive oil
12 green onions, chopped
½ pound cremini mushrooms, chopped
Salt and pepper to taste
8 large eggs
½ cup grated Parmesan cheese

Directions
1. Warm the olive oil in the Dutch oven over medium heat. Add the diced onion and chopped cremini mushrooms.
2. Season with salt and pepper and cook for about 10 minutes.
3. Whisk the eggs and Parmesan together and pour over the cooked mushrooms and onions.
4. Cover and cook for 20–25 minutes at 350°F (180°C).
5. Slice and serve.

Nutrition (per serving)
Calories 278, Fat 20.1 g, carbs 6.9 g,
Protein 19.3 g, sodium 281 mg

Corned Beef Hash Browns

Serves 4 | Prep time 10 minutes | Cooking time 30 minutes

Ingredients
2 tablespoons olive oil
1 onion, diced
2 pounds frozen hash browns
1 teaspoon dried oregano
Salt and pepper to taste
4 cups cooked corned beef, chopped
8 large eggs

Directions
1. Warm the olive oil in the Dutch oven over medium heat. Add the diced onion and hash browns.
2. Season with oregano and salt and pepper to taste. Cook for about 10 minutes. Remove from Dutch oven and set aside.
3. Add the corned beef to the greasy Dutch oven and stir-cook for around 5 minutes until lightly browned.
4. Stir the cooked hash browns and onions back in.
5. Make 8 holes and crack an egg into each hole.
6. Cover and cook for 20–25 minutes at 350°F (180°C).
7. Serve warm.

Nutrition (per serving)
Calories 421, Fat 31.8 g, carbs 5.6 g,
Protein 28.1 g, sodium 1134 mg

Baked Oatmeal

Serves 4 | Prep time 10 minutes | Cooking time 35 minutes

Ingredients
¼ cup butter
2 cups blueberries
3 cups old fashioned oats
2½ cups whole milk
1 cup maple syrup
2 teaspoons baking powder
Pinch of salt

Directions
1. Warm the butter in the Dutch oven and spread the blueberries over the bottom.
2. Sprinkle the old fashioned oats on top of the blueberries.
3. Whisk the whole milk, maple syrup, baking powder, and salt in a medium bowl. Pour over the oats, making sure to cover them completely with the liquid.
4. Cover and cook for 35–40 minutes at 350°F (180°C).
5. Serve warm.

Nutrition (per serving)
Calories 911, Fat 24.6 g, carbs 151.9 g,
Protein 20.6 g, sodium 191 mg

SOUPS

Chicken Mushroom Soup

Serves 8 | Prep. time 10–15 minutes |
Cooking time 30 minutes

Ingredients
2 tablespoons olive oil
2 cups fresh mushrooms, sliced
2 medium carrots, chopped
2 celery ribs, chopped
1 small onion, chopped
1-quart chicken broth
⅓ cup all-purpose flour
2 cups cooked chicken, cubed
1 (8¾-ounce) package precooked chicken-flavored rice
2 cups Fat-free half-and-half
½ teaspoon pepper

Directions
1. Add the oil to the Dutch oven and heat it over medium-high heat.
2. Add the vegetables and stir-cook until the carrots become soft, crisp, and tender.
3. Add the broth and flour to a mixing bowl. Mix well.
4. Pour the broth into the Dutch oven and bring to a boil, stirring occasionally.
5. Stir-cook for 5–6 minutes until thickened.
6. Add the other ingredients and cook over medium-low heat until cooked to satisfaction.
7. Serve warm.

Nutrition (per serving)
Calories 224, Fat 7 g, carbs 23 g,
Protein 15 g, sodium 741 mg

Creme Potato Chicken Soup

Serves 8 | Prep. time 10 minutes | Cooking time 10 minutes

Ingredients
3½ cups water
4 cups shredded cooked chicken breast
2 (10¾-ounce) cans condensed cream of chicken soup, undiluted
1 pound frozen mixed vegetables, thawed
1 (14½-ounce) can potatoes, drained and diced
1 pound Velveeta, cubed
Minced chives (optional)

Directions
1. Add the water, chicken breast, chicken soup, vegetables, and potatoes to the Dutch oven. Bring to a boil.
2. Reduce heat to low, cover, and simmer for 8–10 minutes until the veggies are tender, stirring occasionally.
3. Mix in the cheese.
4. Serve warm with minced chives on top.

Nutrition (per serving)
Calories 429, Fat 22 g, carbs 23 g,
Protein 33 g, sodium 1464 mg

Beef and Cabbage Soup

Serves 10 | Prep time 15 minutes | Cooking time 2 hours

Ingredients
1 pound beef stew meat, cut into ¾-inch pieces
Salt and pepper
2 tablespoons olive oil
6 cups beef stock, divided
1 medium-sized green cabbage, shredded
6 tomatoes, crushed
1 large onion, diced
3 cups of water
2 cloves garlic, minced
1 ½ teaspoon Italian seasoning

Directions
1. Pat the beef dry with paper towels and season with salt and pepper.
2. Add oil to a large Dutch oven and sear the meat over medium heat on all sides until well browned. Do not overcrowd the oven, work in batches if needed. Place the browned beef on a plate.
3. Add about half of the beef stock and bring to a boil. Stir and scrape the brown bits. Return the beef to the Dutch oven.
4. Add the cabbage, tomatoes, onion, remaining beef stock, water, garlic, Italian seasoning.
5. Bring to a boil over medium-high heat.
6. Decrease the heat to medium-low and let cook for 2 hours until the beef is tender and cabbage soft, taking care of stirring a few times.
7. Taste and adjust seasoning with salt and pepper.

Nutrition (per serving)
Calories 176, Fat 3 g, carbs 15 g
Protein 13 g, Sodium 816 mg

Quinoa Chickpea Corn Soup

Serves 6-8 | Prep. time 10 minutes |
Cooking time 25 minutes

Ingredients
1 tablespoon olive oil
1 medium red onion, chopped
1–2 jalapeño peppers, seeded and chopped (optional)
4 cloves garlic, minced
¼ teaspoon pepper
1 cup red quinoa, rinsed
2 quarts vegetable broth
3 medium tomatoes, chopped
1 cup fresh or frozen corn
2 (15-ounce) cans unsalted chickpeas or garbanzo beans, rinsed and drained
Chopped fresh cilantro (optional)

Directions
1. Add the oil to the Dutch oven and heat it over medium-high heat.
2. Add the onion, jalapeño, and garlic. Stir-cook for 3–5 minutes until softened and tender.
3. Mix in the quinoa and broth.
4. Bring to a boil.
5. Reduce heat to low and simmer for about 10 minutes until the quinoa is tender, stirring occasionally.
6. Mix in the tomatoes, corn, chickpeas, and continue cooking until warm through, about 10 minutes.
7. Serve warm with chopped cilantro on top if desired.

Nutrition (per serving)
Calories 289, Fat 5 g, carbs 48 g,
Protein 13 g, sodium 702 mg

Sweet Potato Soup

Serves 8 | Prep. time 20 minutes |
Cooking time 1 hour 30 minutes

Ingredients
4 sweet potatoes, peeled and diced
1 onion, minced
2 (14-ounce) can of light coconut milk
2 cup vegetable broth
4 cloves garlic, minced
2 teaspoon dried basil
Salt and pepper

Directions
1. Place all the ingredients in the Dutch oven and stir.
2. Cover and cook for 1 hour 30 minutes, or until the sweet potatoes are tender.
3. Puree with an immersion blender until the soup is smooth.

Nutrition (per serving):
Calories 127, Fat 5 g, carbs 20 g
Protein 1 g, sodium 159 mg

Pork and Bean Soup

Serves 8 | Prep. time 15 minutes | Cooking time 55 minutes

Ingredients
1-quart water
3 cups pork roast, cooked and cubed
1 (15-ounce) can navy beans, rinsed and drained
2 medium potatoes, peeled and chopped
1 large onion, chopped
1 (14½-ounce) can Italian diced tomatoes with juices
½ cup unsweetened apple juice
½ teaspoon salt
½ teaspoon pepper
Minced fresh basil (optional)

Note Cook in two batches if needed, or halve the
ingredients to make the soup for 4–5 people.

Directions
1. Add the water, pork roast, beans, potatoes, and
   remaining ingredients to the Dutch oven.
2. Bring to a boil.
3. Reduce heat to low, cover, and simmer, stirring
   occasionally, for 40–45 minutes until the roast is
   cooked to perfection and veggies are tender and
   crisp.
4. Serve warm with minced basil on top.

Nutrition (per 1 cup serving)
Calories 206, Fat 5 g, carbs 23 g,
Protein 18 g, sodium 435 mg

Tomato Cream Soup with Basil

Serves 6 | Prep time 15 minutes | Cooking time 2 hours

Ingredients
3 large carrots, peeled
2 celery stalks
2 medium onions
4 whole cloves garlic, peeled
4 (28-ounce) cans whole peeled tomatoes
1-quart chicken broth, low sodium
½ cup fresh basil leaves, roughly chopped, more for serving
Salt and pepper to taste
⅓ Cup heavy cream

Directions:
1. Dice the carrots, celery, and onions.
2. Combine the carrots, celery, onions, garlic, tomatoes, chicken broth, and basil in the Dutch oven.
3. Bring to a boil, cover, reduce heat to low, and cook for 2 hours or until the vegetables are soft and tender. The tomatoes should be soft and easy to puree.
4. Use an immersion blender to puree.
5. Add the cream and blend it in. Season to taste with salt and pepper.
6. Serve garnished with more basil leaves, if desired.

Nutrition (per serving)
Calories 180, Fat 5 g, carbs 31 g
Protein 5 g, sodium 470 mg

Chicken Bean Barley Soup

Serves 8 | Prep time 15 minutes | Cooking time 3 hours

Ingredients

2 strips thick-cut bacon
1 large onion, diced
2 cloves garlic, minced
1 cup dried barley, soaked overnight, rinsed, and drained
1 ½ cups dried navy beans, soaked overnight, rinsed, and drained
6 cups low sodium chicken *broth*
4 cups of water
1 pound spinach, washed and roughly chopped
1 small rotisserie chicken, skin removed, and meat shredded
Salt and pepper to taste

Directions

1. Brown the bacon in the Dutch oven over medium heat. When crisp, drain and transfer to a plate lined with paper towels. Set aside.
2. Drain off the drippings, leaving about 1 tablespoon. Sauté the onion and garlic until tender.
3. Place the barley and beans in the Dutch oven.
4. Pour in the broth and water, and stir.
5. Bring to a boil over medium-high heat. Cover, reduce heat to medium-low and cook 60-75 minutes until beans and barley are tender. Check a few times and add more water if needed.
6. Add the spinach and chicken continue cooking for another 20 minutes.
7. Crumble the reserved bacon. Serve warm with some of the bacon on top.

Nutrition (per serving)

Calories 149, Fat 3 g, carbs 15g
Protein 16 g, Sodium 392 mg

Collard Green White Bean Soup with Sausages

Serves 6 | Prep time 10 minutes | Cooking time 2-2 ½ hours

Ingredients:
1 pound dried white beans, soaked overnight, rinsed, and drained
Water
Salt and pepper
½ pound Cajun Andouille sausages, sliced
1/2 large onion, chopped
2 stalks celery, chopped
4 sprigs fresh thyme
8 cups chicken broth, low-sodium
8 cups collard greens, leaves only, cut into 1-inch pieces
1 tablespoon red wine vinegar

Directions
1. Place the beans in a Dutch oven and cover with water. Season with salt and pepper.
2. Bring to a boil over high heat. Reduce heat to medium-low, cover, and cook for 45-50 hours or until the beans are tender. Remove from heat and drain the water.
3. Add the sausages, onion, celery, thyme, and chicken broth. Bring a boil over high heat, reduce heat to low, cover and cook for 30 minutes over medium-low heat.
4. Remove the thyme stems and drop in the collard greens. Cover and cook 15-20 minutes longer or until the greens are tender.
5. Add the vinegar, and season with salt and pepper to taste.

Nutrition (per serving)
Calories 393, Fat 8 g, carbs 51 g
Protein 30 g, sodium 670 mg

Bacon and Potato Soup

Serves 8 | Prep time 15 minutes |
Cooking time 60-70 minutes

Ingredients
8 strips bacon
2 teaspoons bacon drippings or olive oil
1 large onion, chopped
3 pounds potatoes, peeled, cut into ¼-inch slices
1 cup of water
2 (14 ½-ounce) cans chicken broth, Fat-free, lower-sodium
½ teaspoon salt
½ teaspoon freshly ground black pepper
2 cups low-Fat milk
¾ cup cheddar cheese, shredded, more for serving

For serving
½ cup light sour cream (optional)
4 teaspoons fresh chives, chopped (optional)

Directions
1. Fry the bacon strips in the Dutch oven until crispy over medium heat, about 4-5 minutes. Remove the bacon and place on a plate lined with paper towels.
2. Keep about 2 tablespoons of the bacon drippings (or oil) in the Dutch oven. Add olive oil if necessary. Warm the drippings over medium heat, and stir-fry the onions until tender. Remove from heat.
3. Place the potato slices in the Dutch oven. Stir in the water, broth, salt, and pepper, and stir.
4. Cover and cook for 40-45 minutes over medium-low heat or until the potatoes are tender.
5. Mash potatoes with a potato masher or blender stick. Stir in milk and cheese. Stir to combine.
6. Let simmer over low heat for about 20-25 minutes or until heated through and smooth.

7. Serve with sour cream, sprinkled with bacon, chives, more cheese, if desired.

Nutrition (per serving)
Calories 259, Fat 6 g, carbs 38 g
Protein 13 g, Sodium 683 mg

CHICKEN AND POULTRY

Chicken and Squash One-Pot Meal

Serves 4 | Prep. time 15–20 minutes |
Cooking time 1 hour 30 minutes

Ingredients
1 (3–4 pound) fryer/boiler chicken
2 teaspoons salt
4 cups 1-inch dry bread cubes
2 cups butternut squash, cut into ½-inch cubes
½ large red onion, chopped
4 sprigs fresh thyme

Directions
1. Preheat the oven to 375°F (190°C). Place a rack in the lower third.
2. Pat the chicken dry and season evenly with salt.
3. Layer the bread cubes and squash over the bottom of the Dutch oven. Add the thyme on top.
4. Make a well in the center of the Dutch oven and place the chicken in the well. Insert a cooking thermometer in its thigh.
5. Cover and bake for 1 hour.
6. Remove the lid and continue to bake for 30 more minutes until the chicken is golden, tender, and crisp. The juices should run clear and the cooking thermometer should read 165°F.
7. Let cool for a while and then shred the meat.
8. Serve with the cooked squash and bread mixture.

Nutrition (per serving)
Calories 992, Fat 61 g, carbs 27 g,
Protein 79 g, sodium 1188 mg

Arugula Chicken Spaghetti

Serves 4 | Prep. time 10 minutes | Cooking time 20 minutes

Ingredients
½ pound bucatini or spaghetti
2 tablespoons butter
1 cup Parmesan cheese, grated
2 cups warm rotisserie chicken, diced
4 cups baby arugula
Salt and pepper to taste
Grated Parmesan cheese for serving

Directions
1. Boil salted water in the Dutch oven and cook the spaghetti until cooked well. Drain and set aside. Reserve 1¼ cups of the pasta water.
2. Add the butter and some pepper to the Dutch oven and melt the butter over medium-high heat for about 1 minute.
3. Pour in the pasta water and simmer. Mix in the Parmesan and cooked pasta. Season with salt and pepper.
4. Simmer over low heat until the cheese melts.
5. Mix in the chicken and arugula; stir-cook until the arugula is wilted.
6. Serve warm with grated Parmesan cheese.

Nutrition (per serving)
Calories 596, Fat 23 g, carbs 62 g,
Protein 36 g, sodium 573 mg

Artichoke Potato Chicken Legs

Serves 4 | Prep. time 10–15 minutes |
Cooking time 70–75 minutes

Ingredients
4 chicken leg quarters
Salt and pepper to taste
2 teaspoons coriander seeds, crushed
¼ cup olive oil
⅓ cup dry white wine
⅓ cup chicken stock
1 pound fingerling potatoes
3 strips lemon zest
1 (14-ounce) can unseasoned artichoke hearts, drained and halved
1 cup peas, fresh or frozen
1 tablespoon unsalted butter, cut into pieces
2 tablespoons fresh mint, chopped

Directions
1. Preheat the oven to 350°F (175°C).
2. Season the chicken quarters evenly with salt, pepper, and coriander seeds.
3. Add the oil to the Dutch oven and heat it over medium-high heat.
4. Add the chicken quarters and stir-cook for 6–8 minutes until evenly browned. Cook in batches if needed. Set aside.
5. Pour the wine into the Dutch oven and cook for 1–2 minutes.
6. Mix in the potatoes, lemon zest, and stock, and then add the chicken, skin side up.
7. Cover and bake for 35–40 minutes until the chicken is cooked well and the potatoes are softened.
8. Add the peas and artichoke hearts; cover and bake for 8–10 minutes until the peas are tender.
9. Mix in the butter and serve warm with mint on top.

Nutrition (per serving)
Calories 336, Fat 21 g, carbs 29 g,
Protein 26 g, sodium 485 mg

Cheesy Baked Chicken Spaghetti Casserole

Serves 8 | Prep. time 15–20 minutes |
Cooking time 55 minutes

Ingredients
4 bone-in chicken thighs with skin
1 teaspoon Italian seasoning
Salt and pepper to taste
1 dash balsamic vinegar
1 pound Italian sausages
½ pound mushrooms, sliced
3 cups spaghetti sauce
1 pound spaghetti
2 cups shredded Italian cheese blend

Directions
1. Preheat the oven to 350°F (175°C).
2. Boil salted water in the Dutch oven and cook the spaghetti partially for 4 minutes. Drain and set aside.
3. Spray the Dutch oven with cooking spray and heat it over medium-high heat.
4. Add the chicken thighs and stir-cook for 3 minutes per side until evenly browned.
5. Season with salt, Italian seasoning, and pepper. Transfer to a plate and sprinkle vinegar on top.
6. Add the sausage and mushrooms to the Dutch oven; stir-cook for 4–5 minutes until evenly browned. Drain and remove residual grease.
7. Add the spaghetti sauce and cooked chicken (skin side up) to the Dutch oven.
8. Cook for 3–5 minutes until the sauce is bubbly.
9. Cover and bake for 30 minutes.

10. Add the spaghetti noodles and Italian cheese blend on top; bake for 10 more minutes until cooked to satisfaction.
11. Serve warm.

Nutrition (per serving)
Calories 614, Fat 27 g, carbs 58 g,
Protein 33 g, sodium 1112 mg

Enchilada Penne Chicken

Serves 6 | Prep. time 10 minutes | Cooking time 25 minutes

Ingredients
2 tablespoons olive oil
½ small sweet onion, chopped
2 cloves garlic, minced
2 large chicken breasts, diced
1 tablespoon taco seasoning
2 (10-ounce) cans red enchilada sauce (you can also use homemade enchilada sauce)
2 cups chicken broth
½ pound penne pasta
1½ cups shredded cheddar cheese
Chopped cilantro or chopped green onions for garnish (optional)

Directions
1. Add the oil to the Dutch oven and heat it over medium-high heat.
2. Add the onion and stir cook for 1 minute until softened and translucent.
3. Add the garlic and stir cook for 3–4 minutes until fragrant.
4. Add the diced chicken and taco seasoning and stir-cook until cooked through.
5. Mix in the chicken broth, enchilada sauce, and noodles.
6. Bring to a boil.
7. Reduce heat to low, cover, and simmer for about 10 minutes.
8. Uncover and simmer the mixture for about 10 minutes, until the noodles are cooked well and the sauce is reduced to half.
9. Remove from heat and mix in 1 cup of the cheese until melted.

10. Top with the remaining ½ cup of cheese and serve with chopped cilantro or chopped green onions on top.

Nutrition (per serving)
Calories 383, Fat 16 g, carbs 35 g,
Protein 20 g, sodium 838 mg

Salsa Verde Chicken

Serves 4 | Prep. time 10 minutes |
Cooking time 30–45 minutes

Ingredients
4 boneless, skinless chicken breasts
Salt and pepper to taste
1 chopped red onion
1 jar salsa verde
2 teaspoons ground cumin

Directions
1. Season the chicken breasts evenly with salt and pepper.
2. Arrange the chicken breasts over the bottom of the Dutch oven.
3. Top with the onion, salsa, and cumin.
4. Cover and cook for 30–45 minutes until the chicken is easy to shred.
5. Remove the chicken, shred it, and mix it back into the sauce.
6. Serve warm with cilantro on top.

Nutrition (per serving)
Calories 244, Fat 3 g, carbs 4 g,
Protein 26 g, sodium 1384 mg

Olive Chicken

Serves 4 | Prep. time 10 minutes |
Cooking time 50–60 minutes

Ingredients
6–8 boneless, skinless chicken thighs
Salt and pepper to taste
1 cup pitted olives (green or black)
½ cup low-sodium chicken broth
¼ cup unsalted butter
Lemon juice to taste

Directions
1. Season the chicken breasts evenly with salt and pepper.
2. Arrange the chicken thighs over the bottom of the Dutch oven.
3. Top with broth, butter, and olives.
4. Cover and cook for 50–60 minutes until the chicken is tender.
5. Mix in some lemon juice and serve warm.

Nutrition (per serving)
Calories 542, Fat 18 g, carbs 8 g,
Protein 19 g, sodium 1247 mg

Spiced Chicken Wings

Serves 8 | Prep. time 10–15 minutes |
Cooking time 60 minutes

Ingredients
16 chicken wings (about 3 pounds)
¾ cup bottled plum sauce
1 tablespoon butter, melted
1 teaspoon five-spice powder
Green onions, slivered (optional)

Directions
1. Preheat the oven to 375°F (190°C). Line a 15×10-inch baking pan with foil.
2. Cut the tips off the wings and slice the wings into halves.
3. Arrange the wings over the baking pan and bake for 20 minutes. Drain.
4. Add the plum sauce, butter, and five-spice powder to the Dutch oven.
5. Add the chicken wings and stir to coat well.
6. Cover and cook for 50–60 minutes until the chicken is tender.
7. Serve warm with some slivered green onions on top.

Nutrition (per serving)
Calories 378, Fat 8 g, carbs 45 g,
Protein 27 g, sodium 1355 mg

Parmesan Mushroom Chicken

Serves 4 | Prep. time 15 minutes |
Cooking time 1–1½ hours

Ingredients
6–8 bone-in, skin-on chicken thighs
Salt and pepper to taste
1 Parmesan rind
1 garlic head, halved
½ cup low-sodium chicken broth
½ pound cremini mushrooms, quartered

Directions
1. Season the chicken thighs evenly with salt and pepper.
2. Arrange the chicken thighs over the bottom of the Dutch oven.
3. Add the Parmesan rind, garlic, and chicken broth.
4. Cover and cook for 1–1½ hours until the chicken is tender.
5. Remove the chicken, shred it, and mix it back into the sauce.
6. Serve warm with grated Parmesan on top.

Nutrition (per serving)
Calories 228, Fat 13 g, carbs 7 g,
Protein 23 g, sodium 1160 mg

Roasted Chicken and Potatoes

Serves 4 | Prep time 10 minutes | Cooking time 60 minutes

Ingredients
1 (4-pound) whole chicken
Salt and pepper to taste
4 cloves garlic, minced
5 tablespoons butter, softened
2 tablespoons basil, freshly chopped
Juice and zest of 1 lemon
1½ pounds baby potatoes

Directions
1. Preheat the oven to 450°F (220°C).
2. Wash the chicken and pat dry with paper towels.
3. Season with salt and pepper.
4. Mix the butter with the freshly chopped basil and lemon zest.
5. Brush the chicken with the butter, rubbing it under the skin with your hands.
6. Place the lemon juice inside the chicken. Crush the garlic and place it inside the chicken as well.
7. Arrange the baby potatoes in the Dutch oven. Sprinkle with butter and season with salt and pepper.
8. Place the whole chicken in the center of the Dutch oven.
9. Cover and bake for 20–25 minutes.
10. Remove the lid and reduce the heat to 350°F (180°C). Bake uncovered for about 40 minutes.
11. Serve warm.

Nutrition (per serving)
Calories 1097, Fat 48.3 g, carbs 23.6 g,
Protein 136.1 g, sodium 510 mg

Turkey Meatballs in Tomato Sauce

Serves 4 | Prep time 10 minutes | Cooking time 20 minutes

Ingredients
2 pounds ground turkey
Salt and pepper to taste
1 egg yolk
¼ cup breadcrumbs
¼ cup grated Parmesan cheese
3 tablespoons butter
2 cups tomato sauce

Directions
1. Add the ground turkey to a large mixing bowl and season with salt and pepper.
2. Stir in the egg yolk, breadcrumbs, and Parmesan.
3. Mix well with your hands.
4. With wet hands, form Ping-Pong-ball-sized meatballs.
5. Warm the butter in the Dutch oven over medium heat. Add the meatballs.
6. Cook for about 5 minutes on each side.
7. Cover and cook for about 5 more minutes to reduce the juices.
8. Pour in the tomato sauce and cook for 10 more minutes uncovered.
9. Serve warm.

Nutrition (per serving)
Calories 455, Fat 24.9 g, carbs 11.7 g,
Protein 48.4 g, sodium 933 mg

Chicken Fajitas

Serves 4 | Prep time 10 minutes | Cooking time 20 minutes

Ingredients
3 tablespoons olive oil
3 bell peppers
1 pound chicken boneless breasts
½ onion cut into half-moons
4 8-inch flour tortillas
¼ cup sour cream
Salt and pepper to taste

Directions
1. Warm the Dutch oven over medium heat and pour in the olive oil.
2. Dice the bell peppers and cut the chicken into strips.
3. Cook the onion in the hot oil for 2 minutes until tender and then stir in the peppers and chicken.
4. Cook for about 10 minutes.
5. Season with salt and pepper.
6. Serve on tortillas topped with a dollop of sour cream and sprinkled with pepper.

Nutrition (per serving)
Calories 418, Fat 22.3 g, carbs 19.3 g,
Protein 35.6 g, sodium 117 mg

One-Pot Chicken Parmesan Spaghetti

Serves 4 | Prep time 5 minutes | Cooking time 15 minutes

Ingredients
2 tablespoons olive oil
1 pound chicken breast, diced into 1-inch pieces
Salt and pepper to taste
1 pound spaghetti
2½ cups marinara sauce
2 cups of water
1 cup grated Parmesan cheese
1½ teaspoons Italian seasoning

Directions
1. Add the olive oil to the Dutch oven and heat over medium heat.
2. Add the chicken pieces and season with salt and pepper.
3. Stir in the spaghetti, marinara sauce, water, and Italian seasoning.
4. Bring to a boil and reduce the heat to low.
5. Cover and cook for 10–15 minutes until all the liquid is absorbed.
6. Stir in the Parmesan.
7. Serve in bowls with a drizzle of olive oil and an extra sprinkle of Italian seasoning.

Nutrition (per serving)
Calories 747, Fat 23.2 g, carbs 84.8 g,
Protein 48.7 g, sodium 992 mg

Crispy Fried Chicken Thighs

Serves 4 | Prep time 10 minutes | Cooking time 15 minutes

Ingredients
½ cup buttermilk
2 teaspoons dried paprika (divided)
Salt and pepper to taste
2 pounds chicken thighs
1 cup + ½ teaspoon all-purpose flour
¼ cup olive oil
1 teaspoon dried garlic
¼ cup of water

Directions
1. Add the buttermilk to a medium mixing bowl. Stir in 1 teaspoon of the paprika and season with salt and pepper.
2. Place the chicken thighs in the buttermilk mixture and let them sit for 5 minutes.
3. On a plate, mix the 1 cup of flour, salt, and pepper to taste, the remaining 1 teaspoon of paprika, and the garlic.
4. Warm the olive oil in the Dutch oven over medium heat.
5. Shake excess liquid off the chicken thighs and coat them with the flour mixture.
6. Fry the chicken thighs fry in the heated oil for about 8 minutes on each side.
7. Remove the chicken thighs and stir in the ½ teaspoon of flour. Cook for 1 minute.
8. Stir in the water and whisk with a wire whisk until a creamy sauce/gravy develops.
9. Serve the sauce on top of the fried chicken thighs.

Nutrition (per serving)
Calories 665, Fat 29.8 g, carbs 25.3 g,
Protein 69.8 g, sodium 228 mg

Creamy Parmesan Chicken with Mushroom Sauce

Serves 4 | Prep time 10 minutes | Cooking time 25 minutes

Ingredients
3 tablespoons butter
1½ pounds chicken breast
Salt and pepper to taste
1 pound mushrooms, diced
2 cloves garlic, minced
1 cup heavy cream
½ cup grated Parmesan cheese

Directions
1. Warm the butter in the Dutch oven over medium heat.
2. Season the chicken breast with salt and pepper to taste.
3. Add the diced mushrooms to the Dutch oven. Season with salt and pepper and cook for 7–10 minutes.
4. Remove the mushrooms and cook the chicken breast for 7–10 minutes on each side.
5. Return the mushrooms to the Dutch oven and stir in the garlic.
6. Pour in the heavy cream and cook for 5 minutes.
7. Just before serving, sprinkle the Parmesan on top, cover, and let sit for 5 minutes.

Nutrition (per serving)
Calories 401, Fat 24.4 g, carbs 5.1 g,
Protein 40.5 g, sodium 169 mg

Creamy Chicken and Rice

Serves 4 | Prep time 10 minutes | Cooking time 30 minutes

Ingredients
3 tablespoons butter
1 pound chicken breast, diced into 1-inch pieces
Salt and pepper to taste
1 cup arborio rice
3 cups of water
½ cup white wine
½ cup grated Parmesan cheese
¼ cup parsley, freshly chopped

Directions
1. Warm the butter in the Dutch oven over medium heat.
2. Season the chicken breast with salt and pepper to taste.
3. Cook for 5 minutes on each side.
4. Stir in the rice and season with salt and pepper.
5. Stir in the wine and water and bring to a boil.
6. Reduce the heat to low and cook, covered, for 20–25 minutes without opening the lid.
7. Stir in the Parmesan cheese and freshly chopped parsley.
8. Serve in bowls.

Nutrition (per serving)
Calories 414, Fat 12.5 g, carbs 39 g,
Protein 28.5 g, sodium 164 mg

Lemony Chicken in Garlic Butter Sauce

Serves 4 | Prep time 10 minutes | Cooking time 30 minutes

Ingredients
¼ cup butter
1½ pounds chicken breast
Salt and pepper to taste
3 cloves garlic, minced
Zest and juice of 1 lemon
¼ cup white wine
1 bunch thyme sprigs

Directions
1. Warm the butter in the Dutch oven over medium heat.
2. Season the chicken breast with salt and pepper to taste.
3. Cook for 8 minutes on each side.
4. Stir in the garlic, lemon zest and juice, and thyme.
5. Pour in the wine and cook until it reduces almost to half and a creamy, lemony sauce forms. It will take around 7 minutes.
6. Serve the chicken pieces drizzled with the lemony sauce.

Nutrition (per serving)
Calories 316, Fat 15.8 g, carbs 2.5 g,
Protein 36.5 g, sodium 170 mg

One-Pot Turkey Mexican Pasta

Serves 4 | Prep time 5 minutes | Cooking time 20 minutes

Ingredients
2 tablespoons butter
1 pound ground turkey
Salt and pepper to taste
1 teaspoon garlic powder
3 cups pasta shells
3 cups of water
1½ cups salsa
1 cup shredded cheddar cheese

Directions
1. Warm the butter in the Dutch oven over medium heat.
2. Add the ground turkey, season with salt and pepper, and cook for about 5 minutes.
3. Add the garlic powder and stir.
4. Add the pasta shells and pour in the salsa and water.
5. Bring to a boil, cover, and cook for 10–15 minutes.
6. Stir in the grated cheese before serving.

Nutrition (per serving)
Calories 691, Fat 30 g, carbs 59.5 g,
Protein 50.6 g, sodium 953 mg

Chicken Pot Pie

Serves 4 | Prep time 10 minutes | Cooking time 40 minutes

Ingredients
2 tablespoons butter
1 medium onion, diced
1 (14-ounce) bag of frozen vegetables
4 cups shredded chicken
Salt and pepper to taste
2 cups whole milk
2 tablespoons flour
1 (12-ounce) can of biscuits

Directions
1. Warm the butter in the Dutch oven over medium heat.
2. Add the diced onion and frozen vegetables and cook for about 5 minutes.
3. Stir in the shredded chicken and season with salt and pepper.
4. Sprinkle with the flour and pour in the milk. Once a creamy sauce develops, remove from heat.
5. Place the biscuits on top and bake at 350°F (180°C) for 25–30 minutes.
6. Serve warm.

Nutrition (per serving)
Calories 736, Fat 28.2 g, carbs 65.3 g,
Protein 53.4 g, sodium 1109 mg

BEEF, PORK, AND LAMB

Beef Roast and Potato

Serves 8 | Prep. time 15–20 minutes | Cooking time 4 hours

Ingredients
½ pound thick-cut bacon, coarsely chopped
1 (4–5 pound) beef chuck roast
Salt and pepper to taste
1 yellow onion, minced
3 sprigs thyme or rosemary
½ cup dry red wine
2 cups beef broth
1 pound small potatoes, halved
½ pound carrots, peeled and cut into 2-inch pieces

Directions
1. Preheat the oven to 325°F (160°C).
2. Season the meat with salt and pepper.
3. Heat the Dutch oven over medium-high heat.
4. Add the bacon and cook until crisp. Drain over paper towels and set aside. Discard the drippings.
5. Place the chuck roast in the Dutch oven and spray with some cooking spray.
6. Cook for 5–6 minutes per side until evenly browned. Set aside.
7. Keep 1 tablespoon of Fat in the Dutch oven.
8. Reduce heat to medium and add the onion, salt, and pepper.
9. Stir-cook for 4–6 minutes until softened and light brown.
10. Pour in the wine and stir-cook until reduced to half.
11. Mix in the broth and thyme/rosemary.
12. Return the beef to the Dutch oven and stir to coat well. Bring it to a simmer.
13. Cover and bake for about 3 hours.

14. Add the bacon, potatoes, and carrots around the roast. Season the veggies with salt and pepper.
15. Bake for 1 more hour until the veggies are tender.
16. Set aside to settle for 15 minutes.
17. Slice and serve warm with braised liquid on top.

Nutrition (per serving)
Calories 728, Fat 48 g, carbs 19 g,
Protein 59 g, sodium 1221 mg

Braised Beef Ribs

Serves 4 | Prep. time 10–15 minutes |
Cooking time 2½ hours

Ingredients
3 pounds bone-in beef short ribs
2 tablespoons vegetable oil
Salt and pepper to taste
1 large onion, sliced
4 cloves garlic, minced
3 cups cooking liquid (wine, beer, or low-sodium broth)
3–4 sprigs fresh rosemary or thyme

Directions
1. Coat the short ribs with oil and season with salt and pepper.
2. Add the ribs to the Dutch oven and heat it over medium-high heat.
3. Stir-cook for 7–8 minutes per side until evenly brown.
4. Add the onion and garlic; stir-cook for 4–5 minutes until softened and fragrant.
5. Add the cooking liquid and bring to a simmer.
6. Add the herb sprigs.
7. Cover and cook over medium heat for about 2 hours until the meat flakes easily.
8. Set aside for 20 minutes to settle.
9. Serve warm with onion sauce on top.

Nutrition (per serving)
Calories 1412, Fat 130 g, carbs 7 g,
Protein 50 g, sodium 1310 mg

Dutch Oven Corned Beef

Serves 8 | Prep. time 10 minutes | Cooking time 3 hours

Ingredients
1 (3–4 pound) corned beef brisket with a spice packet, trimmed
1 medium onion, sliced
1 celery rib, sliced
¼ cup butter, cubed
1 packed cup brown sugar
⅔ cup ketchup
⅓ cup white vinegar
2 tablespoons prepared mustard
2 teaspoons prepared horseradish

Directions
1. Add the seasoning pack and beef to the Dutch oven and cover with water.
2. Add the celery and onion. Bring to a boil.
3. Reduce heat to low, cover, and simmer for about 2½ hours until the meat is tender.
4. Drain the liquid and remove the vegetables.
5. Transfer the beef to a shallow greased roasting pan. Set aside to cool.
6. Clean the Dutch oven. Add the butter and melt it over medium-high heat.
7. Add the remaining ingredients; stir and cook for 25 minutes until the sauce is thickened.
8. Slice the beef, pour the sauce over it, and serve warm.

Nutrition (per serving)
Calories 484, Fat 29 g, carbs 35 g,
Protein 22 g, sodium 1708 mg

Braised Pork Ribs

Serves 4–6 | Prep. time 15 minutes | Cooking time 3 hours

Ingredients
3½–4 pounds country-style pork ribs, bone-in (or 2–2½ pounds boneless)
Salt and pepper to taste
3 tablespoons olive oil (divided)
1 large onion, chopped
1 large carrot, diced
3–4 cloves garlic, minced
¾ cup apple cider
¼ cup apple cider vinegar
1 cup chicken broth
2 tablespoons tomato paste
2 bay leaves
½ teaspoon dried thyme

Directions
1. Preheat the Dutch oven to 300°F (150°C).
2. Season the pork ribs with salt and pepper.
3. Add 2 tablespoons of the olive oil to the Dutch oven and heat it over medium-high heat.
4. Add the pork ribs and stir-cook until evenly browned. Set aside.
5. Add the remaining olive oil to the Dutch oven along with the carrot and onion; stir-cook until softened.
6. Add the garlic and stir cook for 1–2 minutes until fragrant.
7. Mix in the pork ribs, thyme and bay leave.
8. To a mixing bowl, add the apple cider, chicken broth, and vinegar, and tomato paste. Mix well.
9. Pour over the pork.
10. Cover and cook for 3 hours until the meat is tender.
11. Season with salt and pepper.
12. Serve warm.

Nutrition (per serving)
Calories 826, Fat 45 g, carbs 20 g,
Protein 81 g, sodium 379 mg

Pork BBQ Burger

Serves 8 | Prep. time 10–15 minutes | Cooking time 2 hours

Ingredients
2–2½ pounds boneless pork shoulder roast, trimmed
Salt and pepper to taste
1 large sweet onion, cut into thin wedges
1 (18-ounce) bottle hot and spicy barbecue sauce
1 cup carbonated beverage (beer or soda)
8 toasted hamburger buns, split, or 16 toasted French
bread slices, baguette-style
Lettuce leaves, sliced tomatoes, pickles, and/or mustard for
topping (optional)

Directions
1. Season the pork roast with salt and pepper.
2. Arrange the onion and pork roast over the bottom of the Dutch oven.
3. Add the barbecue sauce and carbonated beverage.
4. Cover and cook for about 2 hours until the roast is tender.
5. Remove the onion and pork roast, shred, and set aside in a bowl.
6. Trim off the Fat. Add enough of the cooking liquid to the bowl to moisten the shredded roast.
7. Stuff the mixture between hamburger buns and add toppings of your choice.
8. Serve warm.

Nutrition (per serving)
Calories 378, Fat 8 g, carbs 45 g,
Protein 27 g, sodium 1355 mg

Mushroom Sausage Pizza

Serves 8 | Prep. time 10 minutes | Cooking time 20 minutes

Ingredients
1 tablespoon olive oil
1 cup marinara sauce
½ cup fresh mushrooms, sliced
⅓ Cup chopped onion
1 cup Italian cheese blend, shredded
1 pound frozen pizza dough, thawed
½ pound bulk spicy pork sausage, cooked and drained
Red pepper flakes, minced basil, and grated Parmesan
cheese for topping (optional)

Directions
1. Preheat the oven to 450°F (230°C).
2. Warm the Dutch oven in the heated oven for 2–3
   minutes.
3. On a lightly floured surface, roll the dough into a 12-
   inch circle.
4. Fold an 18-inch piece of foil lengthwise into thirds to
   make a sling.
5. Place the crust over the sling and then lower it to the
   bottom of the Dutch oven; brush it with oil.
6. Spread the marinara sauce on top. Add the
   mushrooms, onions, pork, and cheese on top.
7. Bake for about 20 minutes until the crust is light
   brown.
8. Slice and serve warm with toppings of your choice.

Nutrition (per serving)
Calories 273, Fat 13 g, carbs 27 g,
Protein 11 g, sodium 418 mg

Lentil Sausage Pasta

Serves 4 | Prep. time 10 minutes |
Cooking time 18–20 minutes

Ingredients
2 tablespoons olive oil
½ pound sweet Italian sausage, uncooked (optional to remove casings)
¾ pound farfalle pasta, dried
1 cup cooked lentils
1-quart chicken broth
½ cup dry red wine
½ cup of water
Salt and pepper to taste
Grated Parmesan cheese (optional)

Directions
1. Boil some water in the Dutch oven. Add the lentils and cook over medium heat for 18–20 minutes until tender but not mushy. Drain and set aside.
2. Add the oil to the Dutch oven and heat it over medium-high heat.
3. Add the sausage and stir-cook for 3 minutes until evenly browned. Break into pieces with a spatula.
4. Add the lentils, broth, pasta, red wine, and ½ cup water.
5. Bring to a boil and cook for about 14 minutes until the pasta is cooked well. Season with salt and pepper.
6. Serve warm with grated Parmesan on top.

Nutrition (per serving)
Calories 626, Fat 16 g, carbs 84 g,
Protein 30.5 g, sodium 1125 mg

Beef Carrot Meal

Serves 4 | Prep. time 25 minutes |
Cooking time 1½–2 hours

Ingredients
½ cup red wine or water
½ (6-ounce) can tomato pastes with garlic, basil, and oregano
1–1½ pounds boneless beef short ribs, fat trimmed and cut into bite-sized chunks
Salt and pepper to taste
10 cloves garlic, peeled and smashed
1 pound Roma tomatoes, chopped
½ pound fresh baby carrots, peeled and chopped
Fresh basil (optional)

Directions
1. Add the water/wine and tomato paste to a mixing bowl. Mix well.
2. Season the beef chunks with salt and pepper.
3. Add the beef chunks over the bottom of the Dutch oven.
4. Add the garlic, tomatoes, and carrots. Pour in the tomato paste mixture.
5. Cover and cook for 1½–2 hours until cooked to satisfaction.
6. Serve warm with basil leaves on top.

Nutrition (per serving)
Calories 509, Fat 42 g, carbs 15 g,
Protein 19 g, sodium 568 mg

Bacon Ranch Pasta

Serves 4 | Prep. time 10 minutes | Cooking time 20 minutes

Ingredients
6 slices bacon, diced
1 tablespoon olive oil
1 tablespoon butter
3 cloves garlic, minced
2 cups chicken broth
1¼ cups milk
½ pound spaghetti
½ teaspoon pepper
½ cup Parmesan cheese, shredded
¼ cup sour cream
1 tablespoon ranch seasoning mix
Parsley to serve (optional)

Directions
1. Heat the Dutch oven over medium-high heat.
2. Add the diced bacon and cook until crisp. Drain over paper towels and set aside.
3. Clean the Dutch oven; add the oil and heat it over medium-high heat.
4. Add the garlic and stir cook for 1–2 minutes until fragrant.
5. Add the milk, chicken broth, spaghetti, and pepper. Stir and bring to a boil.
6. Reduce heat to low and simmer until the pasta is cooked well, stirring occasionally.
7. Mix in the bacon, sour cream, ranch dressing, and Parmesan.
8. Serve warm with parsley on top.

Nutrition (per serving)
Calories 397, Fat 20 g, carbs 29 g,
Protein 17 g, sodium 864 mg

Zucchini Beef Meal

Serves 4 | Prep. time 5–10 minutes | Cooking time 25 minutes

Ingredients
2 tablespoons dehydrated minced onion
2 cloves garlic, chopped
1 pound lean ground beef
½ teaspoon salt
¼ teaspoon pepper
1 teaspoon ground cumin
1 cup chunky salsa of your choice
2 cups medium fresh zucchini, cut into rounds and then half circles
Fresh cilantro, chopped

Directions
1. Lightly grease the Dutch oven with cooking spray. Heat it over medium-high heat.
2. Add the onion and garlic and stir-cook until softened.
3. Add the ground beef, salt, and pepper and stir cook for 6–8 minutes until evenly browned.
4. Mix in the cumin and salsa.
5. Reduce heat to low, cover, and simmer for about 10 minutes, stirring occasionally.
6. Mix in the zucchini and simmer for 5–10 minutes until the zucchini is tender and softened.
7. Serve warm with chopped cilantro on top.

Nutrition (per serving)
Calories 198, Fat 4.5 g, carbs 10 g,
Protein 26 g, sodium 838 mg

Cheddar Beef Gnocchi Bake

Serves 4 | Prep. time 10 minutes | Cooking time 20 minutes

Ingredients
1½ pounds ground beef
1 pack taco seasoning
2 cups beef broth
2 (16-ounce) packs of gnocchi
1 (15-ounce) can petite tomatoes, diced
1 cup cheddar cheese
Black olives, green onions, and sour cream for topping
(optional)

Directions
1. Lightly grease the Dutch oven with cooking spray. Heat it over medium-high heat.
2. Add the ground beef and stir-cook until evenly browned; drain excess Fat.
3. Mix in the taco seasoning.
4. Add the broth, gnocchi, and tomatoes; stir gently.
5. Bring to a boil.
6. Reduce heat to low and simmer until the sauce is thickened and the gnocchi is tender, stirring occasionally.
7. Mix in the cheese.
8. Serve warm with optional toppings.

Nutrition (per serving)
Calories 555, Fat 43 g, carbs 32.5 g,
Protein 37 g, sodium 757 mg

Pork Chops Potatoes

Serves 6 | Prep. time 10 minutes |
Cooking time 20–30 minutes

Ingredients
Vegetable oil for cooking
6 pork chops
6 potatoes, peeled and thinly sliced
1 onion, sliced
2 cans cream of mushroom soup
Cheddar or Parmesan cheese, shredded, to sprinkle

Directions
1. Add the oil to the Dutch oven and heat it over medium-high heat.
2. Add the pork chops and stir-cook until evenly browned. Discard excess oil.
3. Add the potatoes and onions. Pour on the mushroom soup.
4. Cover and cook for 20 minutes; continue cooking and check every 10 minutes until the pork chops are cooked well.
5. Serve warm with shredded cheddar or Parmesan cheese on top.

Nutrition (per serving)
Calories 291, Fat 10 g, carbs 7 g,
Protein 43 g, sodium 459 mg

Bulgur Sausage Bean Meal

Serves 8 | Prep. time 10 minutes | Cooking time 30 minutes

Ingredients
½ cup yellow onion, diced
1 pound ground sausage
½ cup green pepper, diced
¾ cup bulgur wheat
1 teaspoon salt
1 tablespoon chili powder
1 tablespoon cumin, ground
1¾ pounds tomatoes, diced
1½ cup fresh green beans
Chopped cilantro (optional)

Directions
1. Lightly grease the Dutch oven with cooking spray. Heat it over medium-high heat.
2. Add the onion, sausage, green pepper, bulgur, and salt; stir-cook until the sausage is evenly browned.
3. Mix in the chili powder, cumin, tomatoes, and green beans.
4. Reduce heat to low and simmer for 20–25 minutes until the veggies are softened and tender, stirring occasionally.
5. Serve warm with chopped cilantro on top.

Nutrition (per serving)
Calories 248, Fat 15 g, carbs 16 g,
Protein 11 g, sodium 682 mg

Succulent Braised Pork

Serves 4 | Prep time 10 minutes |
Cooking time 180 minutes

Ingredients
2 pounds pork shoulder, cut into 4 large chunks
¼ cup butter
Salt and pepper to taste
¾ pound frozen vegetables
1 teaspoon garlic powder
2 tablespoons all-purpose flour
1 cup red wine
2½ cups water

Directions
1. Preheat the oven to 350°F (180°C).
2. Warm the butter in the Dutch oven on medium heat and brown the pork pieces for about 5 minutes on each side. Season with salt and pepper.
3. Remove the pork pieces and cook the frozen vegetables in the grease for 5 minutes.
4. Stir in the garlic powder and flour and mix well.
5. Return the pork shoulder to the Dutch oven and pour in the red wine and water.
6. Mix until a thick sauce forms. If necessary, season again with salt and pepper.
7. Cover and bake for about 1 hour.
8. Reduce heat to 320°F (160°C) and cook for 90 more minutes.
9. Remove the lid and cook for 30 more minutes uncovered.

Nutrition (per serving)
Calories 885, Fat 60.2 g, carbs 16.3 g,
Protein 55.9 g, sodium 273 mg

Roasted Pork Loin in Mushroom Sauce

Serves 4 | Prep time 10 minutes | Cooking time 50 minutes

Ingredients
2½ pounds pork loin
¼ cup butter
Salt and pepper to taste
1 small onion, diced
1 pound mushrooms, diced
1 teaspoon garlic powder
2 cups white wine
1 cup of water

Directions
1. Preheat the oven to 350°F (180°C).
2. Warm the butter in the Dutch oven over medium heat.
3. Cut the pork loin into smaller pieces and season them with salt and pepper.
4. Brown the pork for 8–10 minutes on each side. Remove it from the Dutch oven.
5. Cook the onion and mushrooms in the grease for about 7 minutes.
6. Season with salt and pepper and garlic powder.
7. Return the pork loin pieces to the Dutch oven and pour in the white wine and water.
8. Bring to a boil and then place the Dutch oven in the oven and bake for about 40 minutes.
9. If the meat gets too brown, cover loosely with the lid, letting the steam slowly escape on one side.

Nutrition (per serving)
Calories 920, Fat 51.3 g, carbs 9.1 g,
Protein 81.5 g, sodium 273 mg

Korean Style Pork Chops

Serves 4 | Prep time 10 minutes | Cooking time 30 minutes

Ingredients
2 tablespoons olive oil
¼ cup of soy sauce
2 tablespoons light brown sugar
½ teaspoon grated ginger
1 tablespoon chili and garlic sauce
2 pounds pork chops
2 tablespoons butter
Salt and pepper to taste

Directions
1. Preheat the oven to 350°F (180°C).
2. Warm the butter and olive oil in the Dutch oven over medium heat.
3. Mix the soy sauce, sugar, ginger, and chili and garlic sauce in a small bowl.
4. Season the pork chops with salt and pepper on each side.
5. Brush the pork chops on one side with the soy sauce mixture place them brushed side down in the warmed Dutch oven to brown them for about 5 minutes. Meanwhile, brush the top side with the soy sauce glaze. Turn them over and cook for about 5 minutes on the other side.
6. Pour the remaining soy sauce liquid into the Dutch oven and cook in the preheated oven for 25–30 minutes.

Nutrition (per serving)
Calories 867, Fat 69.3 g, carbs 6.4 g,
Protein 52.2 g, sodium 1124 mg

Slow Roasted Pork Shoulder with Rosemary

Serves 4 | Prep time 10 minutes | Cooking time 30 minutes

Ingredients
2 tablespoons butter
2 tablespoons olive oil
3 pounds boneless pork shoulder
Salt and pepper to taste
2 teaspoons garlic powder
1 tablespoon chili flakes
1½ pounds of frozen vegetables
2 cups of water
3 sprigs rosemary

Directions
1. Preheat the oven to 350°F (180°C).
2. Warm the butter and olive oil in the Dutch oven over medium heat.
3. Season the pork shoulder with salt and pepper, garlic powder, and chili flakes.
4. Brown the pork shoulder for about 7 minutes on each side.
5. Remove the pork and cook the frozen vegetables for about 5 minutes.
6. Return the pork shoulder, pour in the water, and add the sprigs of rosemary.
7. Cover and cook for 1 hour in the preheated oven.
8. Reduce heat to 320°F (160°C), remove the lid, and cook for 60–70 minutes uncovered.

Nutrition (per serving)
Calories 721, Fat 25.4 g, carbs 25 g,
Protein 94.3 g, sodium 300 mg

Sunday Pork Roast

Serves 4 | Prep time 10 minutes | Cooking time 30 minutes

Ingredients
3 tablespoons olive oil
Salt and pepper to taste
2 teaspoons garlic powder
2 teaspoons onion powder
2 teaspoons dried paprika
3 pounds boneless pork butt
2 pounds baby potatoes
½ cup of water

Directions
1. Preheat the oven to 350°F (180°C).
2. Warm the olive oil in the Dutch oven over medium heat.
3. Season the pork butt with salt and pepper, garlic powder, onion powder, and dried paprika.
4. Brown the pork butt on each side for about 7 minutes.
5. Remove the pork and cook the baby potatoes for about 2 minutes.
6. Place the pork butt in the center of the Dutch oven, pour in the water, and season with salt and pepper.
7. Cover and cook for 60 minutes in the preheated oven.
8. Reduce heat to 320°F (160°C), remove the lid, and cook uncovered for 40 minutes.

Nutrition (per serving)
Calories 890, Fat 33.6 g, carbs 30.8 g,
Protein 112.2 g, sodium 215 mg

Pulled Pork

Serves 4 | Prep time 10 minutes |
Cooking time 100 minutes

Ingredients
3 tablespoons olive oil
3 pounds boneless pork butt
Salt and pepper to taste
1 tablespoon Dijon mustard
½ cup ketchup
2 tablespoons brown sugar
1 (12-ounce) can beer

Directions
1. Preheat the oven to 350°F (180°C).
2. Warm the olive oil in the Dutch oven over medium heat.
3. Season the pork butt with salt and pepper and Dijon mustard. Rub the ketchup all over. Sprinkle with the brown sugar.
4. Brown the pork butt for about 7 minutes on each side.
5. Pour in the beer. Cover the Dutch oven and place it in the preheated oven.
6. Cook for 60 minutes.
7. Reduce heat to 320°F (160°C), remove the lid, and cook uncovered for 40 minutes.

Nutrition (per serving)
Calories 832, Fat 33.4 g, carbs 15.2 g,
Protein 107 g, sodium 574 mg

Classic Beef Stew

Serves 4 | Prep time 10 minutes | Cooking time 40 minutes

Ingredients
¼ cup olive oil
2 medium onions, chopped
2 pounds beef chuck
Salt and pepper to taste
1 pound potatoes, peeled and diced into 1-inch chunks
1 pound carrots, peeled and diced into 1-inch chunks
2 teaspoons Herbs de Provence
1½ quarts water

Directions
1. Warm the olive oil in the Dutch oven over medium heat.
2. Add the diced onion and cook for around 5 minutes until tender, stirring occasionally.
3. Meanwhile, cut the beef chuck into 1–1½-inch chunks.
4. Stir the diced beef into the Dutch oven and cook for about 5 minutes until well browned on all sides.
5. Stir in the potatoes and carrots and cook for 5 more minutes.
6. Season with salt and pepper and Herbes de Provence. Cover and let the flavors marry together.
7. Stir in the water and bring to a boil.
8. Cook for about 40 minutes.
9. Serve warm or store for later use.

Nutrition (per serving)
Calories 688, Fat 28.3 g, carbs 34.1 g,
Protein 72.3 g, sodium 247 mg

Roasted Beef with Veggies

Serves 4 | Prep time 10 minutes | Cooking time 70 minutes

Ingredients
¼ cup butter
2 medium red onions, chopped
1 pound potatoes, peeled and diced into 1-inch chunks
1 pound carrots, peeled and diced into 1-inch chunks
2 pounds beef chuck
Salt and pepper to taste
1 cup red wine

Directions
1. Warm the olive oil in the Dutch oven over medium heat.
2. Add the diced onion and cook for around 5 minutes until tender, stirring occasionally.
3. Stir in the potatoes and carrots and cook for 5 more minutes. Remove the veggies to a plate.
4. Season the whole piece of beef chuck well with salt and pepper. Add it to the greasy Dutch oven and brown it on both sides for about 5 minutes.
5. Return the veggies to the Dutch oven with the meat.
6. Stir in the red wine and bring to boil. Cover and transfer the Dutch oven to a preheated oven at 350°F (180°C) and bake for about 50 minutes.
7. Remove the lid and cook uncovered for another 10 minutes until the wine is almost evaporated.
8. Serve warm.

Nutrition (per serving)
Calories 719, Fat 25.8 g, carbs 35.7 g,
Protein 72.4 g, sodium 321 mg

Braised Short Ribs

*Serves 4 | Prep time 10 minutes |
Cooking time 150 minutes*

Ingredients
3 tablespoons vegetable oil
1 large onion, sliced
4 cloves garlic, minced
3 pounds bone-in beef short ribs
Salt and pepper to taste
3 cups beef broth
4 sprigs rosemary

Directions
1. Warm the vegetable oil in the Dutch oven over medium heat.
2. Add the diced onion and cook for around 5 minutes until tender, stirring occasionally. Stir in the minced garlic and cook for 1 more minute. Season with salt and pepper.
3. Remove the onion and garlic to a plate.
4. Season the short ribs well with salt and pepper. Add them to the greasy Dutch oven and brown them for about 5 minutes on each side.
5. Return the onion and garlic to the Dutch oven with the meat.
6. Stir in the beef broth and bring to a boil. Cover and transfer the Dutch oven to a preheated oven at 350°F (180°C) and bake for 120–150 minutes. The ribs are ready when the meat can be easily pulled from the bone.
7. Let rest for 20 minutes before serving.

Nutrition (per serving)
Calories 1474, Fat 135.2 g, carbs 7.3 g,
Protein 52.6 g, sodium 742 mg

Basic Beef Brisket

Serves 4 | Prep time 10 minutes |
Cooking time 150 minutes

Ingredients
2 tablespoons olive oil
2 large onions, sliced
Salt and pepper to taste
3 pounds beef brisket
2 cups of water
1 cup ketchup
2 tablespoons chili powder
1 tablespoon all-purpose flour

Directions
1. Warm the olive oil in the Dutch oven over medium heat.
2. Add the diced onion and cook for around 5 minutes until tender, stirring occasionally. Season with salt and pepper.
3. Remove the cooked onion to a plate.
4. Season the beef brisket well with salt and pepper. Add it to the greasy Dutch oven and brown it for about 5 minutes on each side.
5. Return the onion to the Dutch oven with the meat.
6. Stir in the water, ketchup, and chili powder and bring to a boil. Cover and cook for 120–150 minutes. Remove the beef brisket to a plate.
7. In a small glass, whisk the flour with a little bit of water to make a slurry.
8. Stir the slurry into the juices in the Dutch oven and whisk until a creamy sauce/gravy forms.
9. Serve the cut brisket with the creamy sauce.

Nutrition (per serving)
Calories 799, Fat 29.1 g, carbs 25.7 g,
Protein 105.7 g, sodium 937 mg

Dutch Oven Chili

Serves 4 | Prep time 10 minutes | Cooking time 40 minutes

Ingredients
2 tablespoons olive oil
1 onion, diced
2 pounds stewing beef, diced
Salt and pepper to taste
1 (30-ounce) can bean and chili mix
1 (15-ounce) can diced tomatoes
7 ounces diced green chilies
½ cup of water

Directions
1. Warm the olive oil in the Dutch oven over medium heat.
2. Add the diced onion and cook for around 5 minutes until tender, stirring occasionally.
3. Stir in the diced stewing beef and season with salt and pepper.
4. Cook for about 10 minutes until well browned.
5. Stir in the bean and chili mix, tomatoes, and green chilies.
6. Pour in the water and cook for 25–30 minutes with the lid on.

Nutrition (per serving)
Calories 753, Fat 31.3 g, carbs 25.4 g,
Protein 88.1 g, sodium 1247 mg

Beef and Broccoli

Serves 4 | Prep time 10 minutes | Cooking time 15 minutes

Ingredients
2 tablespoons olive oil
3 spring onions, diced
1 pound ground beef
3 cups broccoli florets
3 cups cooked rice
Salt and pepper to taste
1 cup teriyaki sauce

Directions
1. Warm the olive oil in the Dutch oven over medium heat.
2. Add the diced spring onion and ground beef. Cook for about 5 minutes.
3. Stir in the broccoli florets and cooked rice.
4. Season with salt and pepper and cook for 2 minutes.
5. Stir in the teriyaki sauce and cook for 2–3 more minutes.
6. Serve warm with a salad on the side.

Nutrition (per serving)
Calories 868, Fat 15.3 g, carbs 127.5 g,
Protein 50.7 g, sodium 2866 mg

Creamy Beef Pasta Recipe

Serves 4 | Prep time 10 minutes | Cooking time 15 minutes

Ingredients
2 tablespoons olive oil
1 pound ground beef
Salt and pepper to taste
1 tablespoon Italian seasoning
1 (28-ounce) can tomato sauce
2 cups of water
1 tablespoon chili flakes
1 pound fusilli pasta

Directions
1. Warm the olive oil in the Dutch oven over medium heat.
2. Add the ground beef and cook for about 5 minutes until browned.
3. Season with salt and pepper and Italian seasoning and stir in the tomato sauce, water, and chili flakes.
4. Mix well and stir in the pasta.
5. Cover and cook for about 15 minutes or until a creamy mixture forms.
6. Stir in the grated cheese and mix well.
7. Serve on plates.

Nutrition (per serving)
Calories 730, Fat 16.8 g, carbs 95.2 g,
Protein 51.7 g, sodium 1119 mg

Beef and Veggies

Serves 4 | Prep time 10 minutes | Cooking time 40 minutes

Ingredients
2 tablespoons olive oil
1 onion, diced
1 pound stewing beef, cut into 1-inch cubes
2 (14-ounce) bags frozen vegetables
1 pound cherry tomatoes, halved
Salt and pepper to taste
1 cup of water
2 teaspoons chopped rosemary

Directions
1. Warm the olive oil in the Dutch oven over medium heat.
2. Add the diced onion and cook for 5 minutes until softened.
3. Stir in the stewing beef and cook for around 7–10 minutes to brown on every side.
4. Stir in the frozen vegetables and cherry tomatoes.
5. Season with chopped rosemary and salt and pepper and pour in the water.
6. Bring to a boil, cover, and cook at 350°F (180°C) for about 20 minutes.
7. Remove the lid and cook uncovered for another 20 minutes. The beef and veggies will get a little browned on top and a thick sauce will form inside the pan.

Nutrition (per serving)
Calories 433, Fat 14.7 g, carbs 33.4 g,
Protein 41.4 g, sodium 153 mg

FISH AND SEAFOOD

Pasta with Clams and Pancetta

Serves 4 | Prep. time 10 minutes | Cooking time 55 minutes

Ingredients
3 tablespoons extra-virgin olive oil
2 ounces pancetta, thinly sliced and chopped
1 medium onion, finely chopped
4 cloves garlic, thinly sliced
¾ teaspoon red pepper flakes, crushed
1 (28-ounce) can whole tomatoes, peeled and crushed
2 cups of water
24 littleneck clams, scrubbed
4 ounces (about 1 cup) ditalini pasta or other short cut pasta
A handful of torn basil leaves (optional)

Directions
1. Add the oil to the Dutch oven and heat it over medium heat.
2. Add the pancetta and stir-cook for 4–5 minutes until it begins to crisp.
3. Add the onion and stir cook for 6–8 minutes until softened.
4. Add the garlic and stir cook for 4–5 minutes until fragrant.
5. Mix in the red pepper flakes.
6. Add the crushed tomatoes.
7. Over medium-high heat, simmer and cook for 12–15 minutes until liquid is reduced to half.
8. Add the water and clams. Cover and simmer over low heat for 8–10 minutes.
9. Uncover and remove the opened clams.

10. Cover again and cook the remaining clams for 15 more minutes. Discard any unopened ones; remove the opened clams.
11. Add the pasta and cook for 8–10 minutes until al dente.
12. Mix the clams back into the Dutch oven. Add the fresh basil if desired.
13. Serve warm.

Nutrition (per serving)
Calories 407, Fat 16 g, carbs 35 g,
Protein 30 g, sodium 414 mg

Beer Mustard Shrimp

Serves 4 | Prep. time 10 minutes |
Cooking time 10–15 minutes

Ingredients
1 cup whole-wheat pastry flour or all-purpose flour
1 teaspoon Dijon mustard
1 cup pale ale or light-colored beer
½ teaspoon salt (divided)
2 tablespoons canola oil
1 pound (13–15 pieces) raw shrimp, peeled and deveined,
tails left on
Pepper to taste

Directions
1. Add the flour, mustard, beer, and ¼ teaspoon of the
   salt to a mixing bowl. Mix well to make a smooth
   batter.
2. Cook shrimp in two batches.
3. Add 1 tablespoon of the canola oil to the Dutch oven
   and heat it over medium-high heat.
4. Dip the shrimp in the batter, holding them by their
   tails.
5. Add the shrimp one at a time and stir-cook for 3–4
   minutes until evenly brown. Drain over paper towels.
6. Repeat with the remaining 1 tablespoon of oil and
   the other half of the shrimp.
7. Season with the remaining salt and pepper.
8. Serve warm.

Nutrition (per serving)
Calories 173, Fat 8.5 g, carbs 6.5 g,
Protein 16 g, sodium 825 mg

Tilapia Nuggets

Serves 6–8 | Prep. time 10–15 minutes |
Cooking time 10–12 minutes

Ingredients
1½ cups all-purpose flour
2 pounds tilapia fillets, cut into bite-sized chunks
1 tablespoon onion powder
2 cups dry pancake mix
1-pint club soda
1 tablespoon seasoned salt
2 cups of vegetable oil
Tartar sauce to taste

Directions
1. Add the flour to a bowl. Coat the fish chunks with flour. Place them over paper towels and set aside for 5 minutes.
2. Add the onion powder, pancake mix, soda, and seasoned salt to a mixing bowl. Mix well to make a smooth batter.
3. Coat the fish chunks with the batter.
4. Add the oil to the Dutch oven and heat it to 400°F (200°C).
5. Add the coated fish chunks and fry for 3 minutes per side until evenly brown.
6. Drain over paper towels and serve warm.

Nutrition (per serving)
Calories 308, Fat 3 g, carbs 42 g,
Protein 28 g, sodium 1198 mg

Lobster Bisque

Serves 4–6 | Prep. time 10–15 minutes |
Cooking time 70 minutes

Ingredients

2 (1-pound) live lobsters
3 tablespoons butter
1 medium onion, chopped
2 medium carrots, peeled and chopped
2 tablespoons tomato paste
2 cloves garlic, minced
¾ cup sherry or white wine
1-quart seafood stock
⅔ cup long-grain rice, uncooked
2 cups heavy whipping cream
1½ teaspoons salt
1 teaspoon pepper
Minced fresh parsley(optional)

Directions

1. Boil 2 inches of water in the Dutch oven. Add the lobsters and cook, covered, for 8 minutes. Remove the lobsters and reserve the water.
2. Remove the meat from the lobsters. Reserve the juice and shells; discard the claws and tail.
3. Add the butter to the Dutch oven and melt it over medium-high heat.
4. Add the onion and carrots and stir-cook for 6–8 minutes until softened and translucent.
5. Mix in the tomato paste and cook for 5 minutes.
6. Add the garlic and stir cook for 50–60 seconds until fragrant.
7. Pour in the wine and cook until the liquid reduces to half.
8. Pour in the seafood stock along with the reserved water, juice, and shells. Reserve the meat.

9. Simmer for 1 hour; strain to remove solids and shells.
10. Heat the strained liquid in the Dutch oven. Add the rice and cook for 25–30 minutes until softened.
11. Puree the rice in a blender until it becomes smooth.
12. Mix in the pepper, salt, and cream.
13. Add the lobster meat and simmer over low heat until cooked well.
14. Season with parsley and pepper.
15. Serve warm.

Nutrition (per serving)
Calories 373, Fat 26 g, carbs 20 g,
Protein 10 g, sodium 942 mg

Baked Salmon with Herbs

Serves 4 | Prep time 10 minutes | Cooking time 35 minutes

Ingredients
2 tablespoons olive oil
1 lemon, sliced
2 bunches of dill
2 pounds salmon fillet
¾ cup white wine
Salt and pepper to taste

Directions
1. Arrange the lemon slices on the bottom of the Dutch oven.
2. Arrange the dill on top of the lemon and place the salmon fillet on top of that.
3. Pour in the white wine and season with salt and pepper.
4. Cover and cook at 350°F (180°C) for about 10 minutes.
5. Remove the lid and continue cooking for another 20–25 minutes.

Nutrition (per serving)
Calories 405, Fat 21.1 g, carbs 3.4 g,
Protein 44.5 g, sodium 106 mg

Baked Trout with Cherry Tomatoes

Serves 4 | Prep time 10 minutes | Cooking time 45 minutes

Ingredients
2 tablespoons olive oil
2 tablespoons butter
1 pound potatoes, sliced
1 pound cherry tomatoes
2 pounds whole trout
Salt and pepper to taste
1 lemon, sliced

Directions
1. Coat the Dutch oven with butter.
2. Arrange the potato slices and cherry tomatoes in the Dutch oven and season with salt and pepper.
3. Bake at 350°F (180°C) for about 20 minutes.
4. Meanwhile, season the cleaned trout with salt and pepper and stuff it with lemon slices.
5. Place the trout on top of the potatoes and cherry tomatoes and drizzle some olive oil on top of the fish.
6. Cover and bake for about 20 minutes more.
7. Remove the lid and cook for another 10 minutes.

Nutrition (per serving)
Calories 597, Fat 29.5 g, carbs 23.6 g,
Protein 58.2 g, sodium 149 mg

Tilapia Cacciatore

Serves 4 | Prep time 10 minutes | Cooking time 30 minutes

Ingredients
2 tablespoons olive oil
2 pounds tilapia fillets
Salt and pepper to taste
2 cups tomato sauce
2 teaspoons Italian seasoning
¼ cup white wine
¾ cup diced Kalamata olives

Directions
1. Warm the olive oil in the Dutch oven over medium heat.
2. Season the fish fillets with salt and pepper. Add them to the heated oil and cook for about 5 minutes on each side.
3. Pour in the white wine and cook uncovered for about 5 minutes.
4. When half of the wine has evaporated, pour in the tomato sauce and season with Italian seasoning.
5. Stir in the diced Kalamata olives and cook, covered, for 15–20 minutes.
6. When the tomato sauce has thickened and the fish is cooked, serve on plates.

Nutrition (per serving)
Calories 302, Fat 10.5 g, carbs 7.7 g,
Protein 43.8 g, sodium 774 mg

Seafood Risotto

Serves 4 | Prep time 10 minutes | Cooking time 40 minutes

Ingredients
2 tablespoons olive oil
2 tablespoons butter
1 onion, diced finely
½ pound frozen seafood mix
1½ cups arborio rice
Salt and pepper to taste
½ cup white wine
3 cloves garlic, minced
1-quart water

Directions
1. Warm the olive oil and butter in the Dutch oven over medium heat.
2. Stir in the onion and cook for about 5 minutes or until tender.
3. Stir in the seafood mix and cook for about 5 minutes.
4. Stir in the rice and cook for 5 more minutes.
5. Season with salt and pepper and pour in the white wine.
6. While stirring constantly, pour in the water, ½ cup at a time, mixing well so the mixture remains creamy but not too watery.
7. The risotto is done when the rice is cooked through.
8. Serve while it's still creamy with a dash of pepper on top.

Nutrition (per serving)
Calories 457, Fat 13.7g, carbs 62.1g,
Protein 13.3 g, sodium 233 mg

Calamari Fra Diavolo

Serves 4 | Prep time 10 minutes | Cooking time 40 minutes

Ingredients
2 tablespoons olive oil
2 pounds fresh squid, cut into rings
Salt and pepper to taste
½ cup red wine
½ cup of water
1 (28-ounce) can tomato sauce
2 teaspoons chili flakes
3 cloves garlic, minced

Directions
1. Warm the olive oil and butter in the Dutch oven over medium heat.
2. Stir in the squid rings and cook for about 5 minutes.
3. Season with salt and pepper and chili flakes.
4. Pour in the wine, water, and tomato sauce.
5. Cover and cook for 30 minutes.
6. When the mixture is almost thick and most of the liquid has evaporated, serve alone or on top of pasta or crusty bread.

Nutrition (per serving)
Calories 344, Fat 10.5 g, carbs 19.3 g,
Protein 38.1 g, sodium 1143 mg

Seafood Stew

Serves 4 | Prep time 10 minutes | Cooking time 40 minutes

Ingredients
2 tablespoons olive oil
1 medium onion, diced
3 cloves garlic, minced
1 (14-ounce) bag of frozen vegetables
2 pounds seafood mix
2 tablespoons tomato paste
Salt and pepper to taste
1-quart water

Directions
1. Warm the olive oil in the Dutch oven over medium heat.
2. Cook the diced onion and garlic for about 5 minutes until tender.
3. Stir in the frozen veggies and seafood and cook for 10 minutes.
4. Stir in the tomato paste and season with salt and pepper.
5. Pour in the water and cook for 30 minutes.
6. Serve with bread if desired.

Nutrition (per serving)
Calories 348, Fat 9.3 g, carbs 22.9 g,
Protein 36 g, sodium 760 mg

VEGETARIAN AND SIDES

Parmesan Risotto

Serves 4–6 | Prep. time 10 minutes |
Cooking time 35 minutes

Ingredients
1 tablespoon unsalted butter
1 large shallot, finely chopped
Pinch of salt
2 quarts low-sodium vegetable or chicken broth, at room temperature
2 cups Arborio, carnaroli, or vialone nano rice
½ cup dry white wine
1 cup Parmesan cheese, finely grated

Directions
1. Add the butter to the Dutch oven and melt it over medium-high heat.
2. Add the shallot and salt and stir-cook for 4 minutes until softened.
3. Mix in the rice until mixed well with the butter. Stir-cook for about 2 minutes until lightly toasted and aromatic.
4. Mix in the wine and simmer for 3 minutes until the wine is almost completely reduced and nearly dry.
5. Pour in the broth ½ cup at a time, stirring with each addition.
6. Cook for 20–30 minutes until the mixture is thickened and the rice is al dente.
7. Add some more butter and cheese, if desired.
8. Serve warm.

Nutrition (per serving)
Calories 465, Fat 11 g, carbs 66 g,
Protein 20 g, sodium 720 mg

Cashew Rice Bowl

Serves 4 | Prep. time 10 minutes | Cooking time 20 minutes

Ingredients
¼ cup butter, cubed
1 cup chopped onion
1½ cups long-grain rice, uncooked
1 cup golden raisins
1 cup diced carrots
1 teaspoon onion salt
3 cups chicken broth
2 cups peas, frozen
1½ cups wild rice, cooked
1 cup salted cashews
¼ cup thinly sliced green onions (optional)

Directions
1. Add the butter to the Dutch oven and melt it over medium-high heat.
2. Add the onion, long-grain rice, raisins, and carrots and stir-cook until softened and tender.
3. Add the onion salt and broth.
4. Bring to a boil.
5. Reduce heat to low, cover, and simmer for about 20 minutes until the rice is tender and the liquid is absorbed, stirring occasionally.
6. Add the wild rice, peas, and cashews; stir and heat through.
7. Serve warm with green onions on top.

Nutrition (per serving)
Calories 287, Fat 11 g, carbs 41 g,
Protein 7 g, sodium 514 mg

All-Time Favorite Mac and Cheese

Serves 10 | Prep. time 5–10 minutes |
Cooking time 30 minutes

Ingredients
3 cups of water
3½ cups whole milk
1 pound elbow macaroni
4 ounces Velveeta, cubed
2 cups sharp cheddar, shredded
½ teaspoon salt
½ teaspoon pepper

Directions
1. Add the water, milk, and pasta to the Dutch oven. Stir and heat over medium-high heat.
2. Reduce heat to medium-low and simmer, stirring occasionally, for 12–15 minutes until the mixture is thickened and the pasta is tender.
3. Mix in the Velveeta and cheese and simmer over low heat until melted.
4. Season to taste with salt and pepper.
5. Serve warm.

Nutrition (per serving)
Calories 344, Fat 14 g, carbs 39 g,
Protein 16 g, sodium 450 mg

Creamy Mushroom Pasta

Serves 4 | Prep. time 10 minutes | Cooking time 15 minutes

Ingredients
2 tablespoons olive oil
¾ pound mixed mushrooms (shiitake, cremini, oyster, etc.), sliced
3 cloves garlic, minced
¾ cup heavy cream
¾ pound dry linguine pasta
1-quart chicken, mushroom, or vegetable broth
Salt and pepper to taste
Grated Parmesan cheese
Fresh thyme leaves (optional)

Directions
1. Add the oil to the Dutch oven and heat it over medium-high heat.
2. Add the mushrooms and stir cook for about 4 minutes until lightly browned.
3. Add the garlic, cream, pasta, and broth, and stir cook for a few seconds.
4. Bring to a boil, and then reduce heat to low and simmer for about 12 minutes, stirring occasionally, until the pasta is cooked well and the mixture is thickened.
5. Season with salt and pepper.
6. Serve warm with thyme and grated Parmesan on top.

Nutrition (per serving)
Calories 607, Fat 26 g, carbs 71 g,
Protein 20 g, sodium 1050 mg

Mascarpone Pumpkin Pasta

Serves 4 | Prep. time 10 minutes | Cooking time 15 minutes

Ingredients
1 cup canned pumpkin puree
1-quart vegetable broth
1 cup of water
¾ pound dry penne pasta
2 teaspoons fresh rosemary leaves, finely chopped
¼ cup mascarpone cheese
¼ teaspoon pepper
Grated Parmesan cheese (optional)

Directions
1. Add the pumpkin puree, broth, water, and pasta to the Dutch oven and bring to a boil over medium-high heat.
2. Reduce heat to low and simmer for 10–12 minutes until most of the liquid evaporates, stirring occasionally.
3. Mix in the mascarpone, rosemary, and pepper.
4. Stir-cook for about 2 minutes until the pasta is cooked to your satisfaction.
5. Serve warm with grated Parmesan on top.

Nutrition (per serving)
Calories 245, Fat 4 g, carbs 43g,
Protein 8 g, sodium 63 mg

Classic Cheesy Spaghetti

Serves 4 | Prep. time 10 minutes | Cooking time 12 minutes

Ingredients
½ cup of water
1-quart chicken broth
¾ pound dry spaghetti
1 Parmesan cheese rind (optional)
¾ cup Pecorino-Romano cheese, grated
2 teaspoons pepper

Directions
1. Add the water, broth, and pasta and Parmesan rind to the Dutch oven and bring to a boil over medium-high heat.
2. Simmer for 8–9 minutes until most of the liquid evaporates, stirring occasionally.
3. Mix in the Pecorino-Romano and pepper.
4. Stir-cook for 2 minutes until the pasta is cooked to your satisfaction.
5. Remove the Parmesan rind.
6. Serve warm.

Nutrition (per serving)
Calories 497, Fat 10.5 g, carbs 73.5 g,
Protein 25 g, sodium 685 mg

Braised Leeks

Serves 6 | Prep. time 15 minutes | Cooking time 50 minutes

Ingredients
6 medium leeks (white portion and light green parts only), halved lengthwise
¼ cup butter
2 garlic cloves, minced
1 teaspoon dry rosemary (or 2 teaspoons fresh rosemary)
1 teaspoon lemon zest, grated
2 teaspoons sugar
½ cup dry white wine
Salt and pepper to taste

Directions
1. Preheat the oven to 350°F (180°C).
2. Clean the leeks under cold running water to remove any remaining dirt.
3. Add the butter in the Dutch oven, and let melt over medium-low heat. Add the leeks and brown them on the cut side down for 2-3 minutes over medium heat.
4. Turn the leeks over, add the remaining ingredients. Stir to combine. Cover and place in the oven. Bake for 35-45 minutes checking midway to turn over the leeks back cut side down. Add a bit of water if needed to prevent the leeks from sticking to the bottom.
5. Remove from the oven once the leeks are tender. If there is lots of cooking juice, you can reduce it on the stove, uncovered, over medium-high heat until most of the liquid has evaporated.

Nutrition (per serving)
Calories 153, Fat 5 g, carbs 18 g,
Protein 3 g, sodium 77 mg

French Onion Pasta

Serves 4 | Prep. time 10 minutes | Cooking time 35 minutes

Ingredients
3 tablespoons olive oil
1½ pounds yellow onions, sliced paper-thin
⅔ Cup water
1-quart low-sodium vegetable or beef broth
¾ pound dry orecchiette pasta
⅓ cup ruby port
2 ounces (about ¾ cup) Gruyere cheese, finely shredded
Salt and pepper to taste

Directions
1. Add the oil to the Dutch oven and heat it over medium-high heat.
2. Add the onion slices and stir-cook for 15–20 minutes until caramelized and dark.
3. Add the water, broth, pasta, and ruby port; stir and cook for 12 minutes until the liquid is evaporated.
4. Mix in the Gruyere. Season to taste with salt and pepper.
5. Serve warm.

Nutrition (per serving)
Calories 520, Fat 12 g, carbs 84 g,
Protein 17.5 g, sodium 1259 mg

Seasoned French Fries

Serves 6 | Prep. time 10 minutes |
Cooking time 50–60 minutes

Ingredients
3 pounds russet potatoes, cut into ½-inch sticks
3 quarts peanut oil
2 teaspoons Old Bay seasoning
Salt and pepper to taste

Directions
1. Add the potato sticks to a bowl and cover with cold water; set aside for 30–60 minutes. Drain and pat dry.
2. Add the peanut oil to the Dutch oven and heat it to 325°F (160°C).
3. In 2–3 batches, fry the potato sticks for 7–9 minutes until golden brown.
4. Drain over paper towels.
5. Increase heat to 400°F (200°C).
6. Return the cooked potato sticks to the Dutch oven in 2–3 batches and fry for 1–2 minutes until deep golden brown.
7. Drain over paper towels.
8. Season with pepper, salt, and Old Bay seasoning.
9. Serve warm.

Nutrition (per serving)
Calories 226, Fat 7 g, carbs 39 g,
Protein 5 g, sodium 397 mg

Buttery Carrots

Serves 8 | Prep. time 10 minutes | Cooking time 10 minutes

Ingredients
1 cup of water
2 pounds carrots cut into 2-inch pieces
⅓ Cup butter
1 medium onion, thinly sliced
2 tablespoons all-purpose flour
2 teaspoons chicken bouillon granules
¼ teaspoon salt
⅛ teaspoon pepper
Minced fresh parsley

Directions
1. Pour 1 inch of water into the Dutch oven.
2. Add the carrots and boil for 6–8 minutes until tender. Drain and set aside.
3. Add the butter and melt it over medium-high heat.
4. Add the onion and stir-cook until softened and translucent.
5. Add the flour, bouillon, salt, and pepper.
6. Bring to a boil and then simmer for about 2 minutes until the mixture is thickened, stirring occasionally.
7. Stir in the carrots.
8. Serve warm with parsley on top.

Nutrition (per serving)
Calories 129, Fat 8 g, carbs 14 g,
Protein 2 g, sodium 416 mg

Baked Garlic and Mushroom Rice

Serves 4 | Prep time 10 minutes | Cooking time 40 minutes

Ingredients
3 tablespoons olive oil
1 medium onion, diced
1 pound mushrooms, diced
3 cloves garlic, minced
Salt and pepper to taste
1½ cups of rice
3 cups of water
½ cup white wine

Directions
1. Warm the olive oil in the Dutch oven over medium heat. Add the diced onion and cook for 5 minutes until softened.
2. Stir in the diced mushrooms and minced garlic.
3. Cook for about 10 minutes and then stir in the rice.
4. Stir-cook for 2 minutes and season with salt and pepper.
5. Pour in the white wine and cook for 2 minutes. Pour in the water, bring to a boil, and cover.
6. Bake at 350°F (180°C) for about 25 minutes.
7. Remove the lid and cook uncovered for 5 minutes until the rice is set and nicely baked.

Nutrition (per serving)
Calories 406, Fat 11.3 g, carbs 63.3 g,
Protein 9 g, sodium 18 mg

Quinoa with Mixed Vegetables and Artichoke Hearts

Serves 4 | Prep time 10 minutes | Cooking time 40 minutes

Ingredients
3 tablespoons olive oil
1 medium onion, diced
2 cloves garlic, minced
1 (14-ounce) bag of frozen vegetables
½ cup artichoke hearts, diced
2 cups quinoa, washed and rinsed
Salt and pepper to taste
1-quart water

Directions
1. Warm the olive oil in the Dutch oven over medium heat. Add the diced onion.
2. Stir in the minced garlic, frozen veggies, and diced artichoke hearts.
3. Cook for 5 minutes and then stir in the quinoa.
4. Season with salt and pepper and cook for 2 minutes.
5. Pour in the water and bring to a simmer.
6. Reduce heat to low, cover, and cook for 20 minutes.
7. Remove the lid and mix everything to fluff up the quinoa with the veggies.
8. Serve on plates.

Nutrition (per serving)
Calories 490, Fat 15.9 g, carbs 72.8 g,
Protein 15.9 g, sodium 67 mg

Dutch Oven Vegetarian Lasagna

Serves 4 | Prep time 10 minutes | Cooking time 40 minutes

Ingredients
5 tablespoons olive oil
3 large onions, diced
4 cups baby spinach
Salt and pepper to taste
½ pound lasagna sheets
1 (28-ounce) can tomato sauce
4 cups grated mozzarella cheese

Directions
1. Warm the olive oil in the Dutch oven over medium heat. Add the diced onion.
2. Stir in the baby spinach and season with salt and pepper.
3. Cook for 5 minutes until the spinach wilts.
4. Stir in the tomato sauce and cook for 5 minutes.
5. Remove from heat and transfer all but a little of the filling to a bowl.
6. Add a layer of lasagna sheets to the Dutch oven.
7. Add a layer of the filling and sprinkle with mozzarella cheese.
8. Repeat at least two more times or until you run out of lasagna sheets and filling.
9. Sprinkle the top with mozzarella cheese and pepper.
10. Cover and bake at 350°F (180°C) for about 20 minutes.
11. Remove the lid and cook uncovered for about 15 more minutes until the mozzarella is golden brown.
12. Let cool slightly, then slice and serve.

Nutrition (per serving)
Calories 490, Fat 24 g, carbs 54.6 g,
Protein 19.3 g, sodium 1238 mg

Cheesy Ravioli Pasta Bake

Serves 4 | Prep time 10 minutes | Cooking time 40 minutes

Ingredients
3 tablespoons olive oil
1 pound mushrooms, diced
4 (9-ounce) packages spinach ravioli
Salt and pepper to taste
1 (24-ounce) jar marinara sauce
½ pound mozzarella cheese, shredded
½ cup Parmesan cheese

Directions
1. Warm the olive oil in the Dutch oven over medium heat. Add the diced mushrooms.
2. Season with salt and pepper and stir in the marinara sauce.
3. Let the flavors marry together and then add the ravioli.
4. Bring to simmer and transfer the Dutch oven to a preheated oven at 350°F (180°C).
5. Bake for 25–30 minutes.

Nutrition (per serving)
Calories 747, Fat 37.4 g, carbs 69.3 g,
Protein 36.1 g, sodium 2030 mg

Vegetarian Jambalaya

Serves 4 | Prep time 10 minutes | Cooking time 35 minutes

Ingredients
2 tablespoons olive oil
1 medium onion, diced
2 cloves garlic, minced
1 (14-ounce) bag of frozen vegetables
2 (16-ounce) cans red beans, drained and rinsed
1 cup long-grain rice
Salt and pepper to taste
1 (28-ounce) can diced tomatoes
½ cup of water

Directions
1. Warm the olive oil in the Dutch oven over medium heat. Add the diced onion and garlic. Cook for 5 minutes or until the onion is tender.
2. Stir in the frozen veggies and cook for 5–7 minutes.
3. Stir in the rice and cook for 2–3 minutes.
4. Stir in the diced tomatoes and water.
5. Mix and bring to a boil.
6. Reduce heat to low and simmer, covered, for 20 minutes.
7. Stir in the red beans and serve warm.

Nutrition (per serving)
Calories 1113, Fat 9.9 g, carbs 202.2 g,
Protein 59.4 g, sodium 489 mg

Vegetable Stew

Serves 4 | Prep time 10 minutes | Cooking time 40 minutes

Ingredients
5 tablespoons olive oil
1 medium onion, diced
2 (14-ounce) bags frozen mixed vegetables
½ pound mushrooms halved
2 potatoes, peeled and cut into 1-inch cubes
Salt and pepper to taste
1 (14-ounce) can tomato sauce
3 cups of water

Directions
1. Warm the olive oil in the Dutch oven over medium heat. Add the diced onion and cook for 5 minutes until tender.
2. Stir in the frozen vegetables, mushrooms, and diced potatoes and cook for 5–7 minutes.
3. Season with salt and pepper and stir in the tomato sauce and water.
4. Bring to a boil and cook for 30 minutes.
5. Remove half of the diced potatoes to a plate and mash them with a fork.
6. Return them to the Dutch oven and stir to thicken the stew.
7. Serve with extra pepper.

Nutrition (per serving)
Calories 400, Fat 18.3 g, carbs 52.5g,
Protein 10.9 g, sodium 605 mg

DESSERTS

Heavenly Peach Cobbler

Serves 6 | Prep. time 5–10 minutes |
Cooking time 20 minutes

Ingredients
½ pack vanilla cake mix
1 cup lemon-lime soda (Sprite/7 Up)
4 cups fruit (peaches, apples, berries, etc.)
2 tablespoons unsalted butter, cold, diced
2 tablespoons sugar (optional)
Whipped cream

Directions
1. Lightly grease the Dutch oven with cooking spray.
2. Add the cake mix and soda to a mixing bowl. Mix well to make a thick batter.
3. Arrange the fruit in the Dutch oven; pour the batter over it.
4. Top with the diced butter and sugar.
5. Heat the Dutch oven to 350°F (175°C).
6. Cover and cook for 20 minutes until the top is golden brown and the juices are bubbling.
7. Serve warm with whipped cream.

Nutrition (per serving)
Calories 282, Fat 6 g, carbs 57 g,
Protein 3 g, sodium 304 mg

Chocolate Cake

Serves 8 | Prep. time 10 minutes | Cooking time 35 minutes

Ingredients
1 (21-ounce) can cherry pie filling
1 (12-ounce) can evaporate milk
1 regular-size pack chocolate cake mix
⅓ cup almonds, sliced
¾ cup butter, melted
Vanilla ice cream (optional)

Directions
1. Heat the Dutch oven to 350°F (175°C). Line it with parchment paper and lightly grease with cooking spray.
2. Add the pie filling and evaporated milk to a mixing bowl. Mix well.
3. Pour it over the Dutch oven and spread evenly.
4. Add the cake mix and almonds on top.
5. Drizzle the melted butter on top.
6. Cover and cook for 35–40 minutes until the cake springs back when prodded.
7. Serve warm with ice cream.

Nutrition (per serving)
Calories 515, Fat 24 g, carbs 68 g,
Protein 7 g, sodium 605 mg

Cherry Clafouti

Serves 8 | Prep. time 10 minutes | Cooking time 30 minutes

Ingredients
¾ pound fresh or frozen and thawed cherries stemmed and pitted
2 large eggs
¼ cup of sugar
½ cup whole milk
1 teaspoon vanilla extract
½ cup all-purpose flour

Directions
1. Preheat the Dutch oven to 400°F (200°C). Evenly spread butter to cover the inside surface.
2. Spread the cherries over the bottom.
3. Whisk the eggs in a bowl. Add the sugar. Mix until well blended and frothy.
4. Add the flour, milk, and vanilla to another mixing bowl. Mix well.
5. Combine the mixtures to make a smooth batter.
6. Pour the batter over the cherries.
7. Cook, uncovered, for 30 minutes until the top is golden brown. Check by inserting a toothpick; it should come out clean. If not, cook for a few more minutes.
8. Serve warm.

Nutrition (per serving)
Calories 92, Fat 2 g, carbs 16 g,
Protein 3 g, sodium 26 mg

Pecan Pralines

Serves 18 pralines | Prep. time 10 minutes | Cooking time 20 minutes

Ingredients
1 cup whipping cream
3 cups light brown sugar
¼ cup butter
2 tablespoons corn syrup
2 cups pecan halves
1 teaspoon vanilla extract
Wax paper

Directions
1. Preheat the Dutch oven to 350°F (175°C).
2. Spread the pecan halves in the Dutch oven and cook for 5 minutes. Stir-cook for another 5 minutes. Set aside.
3. Clean the Dutch oven and add the whipping cream, brown sugar, butter, and corn syrup.
4. Boil over high heat for 4–6 minutes until the sugar melts completely, stirring occasionally.
5. Remove from heat and add the pecans and vanilla; stir for 1–2 minutes. Let cool for a while.
6. Place a spoonful of the mixture on wax paper; allow to firm up for 10–15 minutes.
7. Serve warm.

Nutrition (per praline)
Calories 228, Fat 14 g, carbs 25 g,
Protein 2 g, sodium 31 mg

Quick and Easy Pop Brownies

Serves 8 | Prep. time 10 minutes | Cooking time 45 minutes

Ingredients
1 box brownie mix
1 can soda pop
¾ pound chocolate chips

Directions
1. Line the Dutch oven with parchment paper.
2. Add the brownie mix and soda to a mixing bowl. Mix well until you get a smooth mixture.
3. Pour the batter over the parchment paper. Sprinkle the chocolate chips on top.
4. Heat to 350°F (175°C) and bake for 45–60 minutes until well set. Check by inserting a toothpick; it should come out clean. If not, cook for a few more minutes.
5. Slice and serve warm.

Nutrition (per serving)
Calories 241, Fat 13 g, carbs 35 g,
Protein 2 g, sodium 16 mg

Chocolate Chip Cookies

Serves 24 | Prep. time 10 minutes |
Cooking time 8–10 minutes

Ingredients
1 cup butter, softened
¾ cup granulated sugar
¾ cup packed brown sugar
1 egg
1 teaspoon vanilla
½ teaspoon of sea salt
1 teaspoon baking soda
2¼ cups flour
1–2 cups semisweet chocolate chips

Directions
1. Add the butter and both sugars to a mixing bowl. Mix well.
2. Beat the eggs in another bowl. Add the vanilla. Mix well.
3. Add the sea salt, baking soda, and flour; mix again.
4. Combine the mixtures until smooth.
5. Mix in the chocolate chips.
6. Divide into 24 balls.
7. Line the Dutch oven with parchment paper and lightly grease it with cooking spray.
8. Arrange the balls on the bottom.
9. Cover and cook for 6 minutes. If cookies have turned light brown, take them out. If not, cook for 2–4 more minutes. Do not overcook.
10. Let cool for a while.
11. Serve warm.

Nutrition (per serving)
Calories 220, Fat 11 g, carbs 29 g,
Protein 2 g, sodium 100 mg

Dutch Oven Brownies

Serves 9 | Prep time 10 minutes |
Cooking time 30 minutes

Ingredients
1 box brownie mix
½ cup melted butter
2 large eggs
3 tablespoons water
1 cup of chocolate chips
1 teaspoon vanilla extract

Directions
1. Add the brownie mix to a large mixing bowl and stir in the melted butter, eggs, and water, and chocolate chips until just combined, being careful not to over-mix the batter.
2. Line the Dutch oven with a piece of parchment paper and pour in the brownie mixture.
3. Bake at 350°F (180°C) for 25–30 minutes.
4. Let the brownies cool slightly and then cut into squares and serve.

Nutrition (per serving)
Calories 502, Fat 27 g, carbs 63.2 g,
Protein 5.7 g, sodium 308 mg

Double Chocolate Cake

Serves 8 | Prep time 10 minutes | Cooking time 30 minutes

Ingredients
1 box chocolate cake mix
⅓ cup vegetable oil
¼ cup whole milk
1 cup of chocolate chips
2 cups heavy whipping cream
3 tablespoons powdered sugar
1 teaspoon vanilla extract

Directions
1. Add the cake mix to a large mixing bowl and stir in the vegetable oil, milk, and chocolate chips until just combined, being careful not to over-mix the batter.
2. Line the Dutch oven with a piece of parchment paper and pour in the chocolate cake mixture.
3. Bake at 350°F (180°C) for about 30 minutes.
4. Remove the cake from the Dutch oven and place it on a cooling rack. Let it cool completely.
5. Add the whipping cream, powdered sugar, and vanilla extract to a large mixing bowl and beat with a hand mixer.
6. Cut the chocolate cake in half to create two layers. Spread half of the whipped cream on one layer, cover with the second layer, and decorate the whole cake with whipped cream.
7. If desired, sprinkle with more chocolate chips for better presentation.

Nutrition (per serving)
Calories 594, Fat 36.9 g, carbs 64.5 g,
Protein 6.3 g, sodium 572 mg

Cinnamon Rolls

Serves 8 | Prep time 10 minutes | Cooking time 30 minutes

Ingredients
8 canned cinnamon rolls
2 cups powdered sugar
5 ounces cream cheese, softened
1 teaspoon vanilla extract
Zest of 1 orange

Directions
1. Place a piece of parchment paper in the Dutch oven and arrange the cinnamon rolls on it.
2. Bake at 350°F (180°C) for 30–35 minutes until golden brown.
3. Add the softened cream cheese to a medium mixing bowl and mix it well with the powdered sugar, vanilla extract, and lemon zest.
4. Make sure that the mixture is pourable. If it's too thick, add a little bit of water.
5. Spread the cream cheese mixture on top of the cinnamon rolls while they are still warm.
6. Let cool slightly and then serve with a cup of coffee or chocolate milk.

Nutrition (per serving)
Calories 281, Fat 9.9 g, carbs 46.1 g,
Protein 2.9 g, sodium 282 mg

Verry Berry Swirl

Serves 6 | Prep time 10 minutes | Cooking time 30 minutes

Ingredients
1 (14-ounce) pizza dough
3 cups frozen or fresh mixed berries
¾ cup granulated sugar
½ teaspoon cinnamon
2 tablespoons all-purpose flour
¼ cup powdered sugar for dusting

Directions
1. Roll out the pizza dough into a ¼-inch-thick square.
2. Sprinkle the mixed berries, granulated sugar, cinnamon, and all-purpose flour on top. Ensure that every berry is coated with flour, so a nice thick sauce will form during baking.
3. Roll up the dough with the berries inside and cut diagonally with a sharp knife.
4. Carefully twist both parts of the dough together to make one long braid.
5. Shape the braid into a circle and place it in the Dutch oven on top of a piece of parchment paper.
6. Bake at 350°F (180°C) for 30–40 minutes.
7. Let cool slightly and then dust with powdered sugar when ready to serve.

Nutrition (per serving)
Calories 473, Fat 20.7 g, carbs 68.6 g,
Protein 4.6 g, sodium 319 mg

Peach Cobbler

Serves 4 | Prep time 10 minutes | Cooking time 30 minutes

Ingredients
2 tablespoons butter
6 tablespoons butter, melted
6 peaches, stoned and cut in wedges
1 cup sugar (divided)
1 cup all-purpose flour
1 tablespoon baking powder
½ cup whole milk
Powdered sugar for dusting

Directions
1. Grease the Dutch oven well on every side with the two tablespoons of butter.
2. Arrange the peach slices in the Dutch oven and sprinkle with ¾ cup of the sugar.
3. To a bowl, add the flour, baking powder, melted butter, milk, and remaining sugar.
4. Mix until combined and then use an ice cream scoop to deposit the batter on top of the peaches in the Dutch oven.
5. Bake at 350°F (180°C) for 30–35 minutes.
6. Let cool slightly and then dust with powdered sugar when ready to serve.

Nutrition (per serving)
Calories 615, Fat 25 g, carbs 98 g,
Protein 6.6 g, sodium 180 mg

Apple Crisp

Serves 6 | Prep time 10 minutes | Cooking time 30 minutes

Ingredients
6 apples, cored and cut into wedges
¼ cup of water
1 cup all-purpose flour
½ cup of sugar
¾ cup butter
1 teaspoon cinnamon

Directions
1. Grease the Dutch oven and place the apple wedges in the bottom.
2. Pour in the water and let sit for 5 minutes.
3. Meanwhile, blend the flour, sugar, butter, and cinnamon in a food processor until a crumbly dough forms.
4. Distribute the dough on top of the apples, making sure you fill every hole, and bake, covered, for about 25 minutes at 350°F (180°C).
5. Remove the lid and cook uncovered for another 10–15 minutes until golden brown.
6. Serve warm with a scoop of ice cream.

Nutrition (per serving)
Calories 459, Fat 23.6 g, carbs 63.7 g,
Protein 3 g, sodium 166 mg

All in One Apple Cake

Serves 8 | Prep time 10 minutes | Cooking time 40 minutes

Ingredients
3 apples, cored and cut into wedges
½ cup butter softened
½ cup of sugar
2 large eggs
1¼ cups self-rising flour
½ cup whole milk
Powdered sugar for sprinkling

Directions
1. Grease the Dutch oven with a small piece of butter.
2. Add the butter and the sugar to a large mixing bowl and beat with a hand mixer until fluffy.
3. Stir in the eggs one at a time, mixing well after each addition.
4. Stir in the flour and mix until just combined.
5. Stir in the apple wedges and mix with a spatula.
6. Pour the cake mixture into the buttered Dutch oven and bake at 350°F (180°C) for about 40 minutes.
7. Let the cake cool slightly before serving with a sprinkle of powdered sugar.

Nutrition (per serving)
Calories 290, Fat 13.6 g, carbs 39.8 g,
Protein 4.4 g, sodium 106 mg

Dutch Oven Chocolate Chip Cookies

Serves 4 | Prep time 10 minutes | Cooking time 20 minutes

Ingredients
½ cup butter, melted
¾ cup light brown sugar
2 teaspoons vanilla extract
2 large eggs, room temperature
1½ cups self-rising flour
1 cup of chocolate chips

Directions
1. Grease the Dutch oven with a little bit of butter.
2. Add the melted butter, sugar, vanilla extract, and eggs to a large mixing bowl.
3. Mix until combined and stir in the flour.
4. Mix in the chocolate chips and transfer the cookie dough to the buttered Dutch oven.
5. Bake at 350°F (180°C) for about 20 minutes.

Nutrition (per serving)
Calories 496, Fat 25.6 g, carbs 58.6 g,
Protein 7.7 g, sodium 160 mg

RECIPE INDEX

APPENDIX

Cooking Conversion Charts

1. Measuring Equivalent Chart

Type	Imperial	Imperial	Metric
Weight	1 dry ounce		28g
	1 pound	16 dry ounces	0.45 kg
Volume	1 teaspoon		5 ml
	1 dessert spoon	2 teaspoons	10 ml
	1 tablespoon	3 teaspoons	15 ml
	1 Australian tablespoon	4 teaspoons	20 ml
	1 fluid ounce	2 tablespoons	30 ml
	1 cup	16 tablespoons	240 ml
	1 cup	8 fluid ounces	240 ml
	1 pint	2 cups	470 ml
	1 quart	2 pints	0.95 l
	1 gallon	4 quarts	3.8 l
Length	1 inch		2.54 cm

* Numbers are rounded to the closest equivalent

2. Oven Temperature Equivalent Chart

Fahrenheit (°F)	Celsius (°C)	Gas Mark
220	100	
225	110	1/4
250	120	1/2
275	140	1
300	150	2
325	160	3
350	180	4
375	190	5
400	200	6
425	220	7
450	230	8
475	250	9
500	260	

* Celsius (°C) = T (°F)-32] * 5/9

** Fahrenheit (°F) = T (°C) * 9/5 + 32

*** Numbers are rounded to the closest equivalent

Outdoor Cooking Using Your Dutch Oven

Campers like to use their Dutch oven for cooking outdoors just like the pioneers and explorers of old. There's something special about using the same cookware that your forefathers did in the great outdoors. Imagine cooking cinnamon rolls and cobblers as a welcome break from the usual s'mores and toasted marshmallows. The camp Dutch oven requires coals for heating. Here are some guidelines:

- Arrange the coals or briquettes in a circular pattern, around the bottom edge of the pot and on the lid. Coals do not need to be placed at the center, except for a large Dutch oven with a 16-inch diameter. For large Dutch ovens, use a checkerboard pattern.

- Rotate the pot and the lid every few minutes to ensure even heating.

- For baking and roasting, more coals are placed on top to keep the food from burning at the bottom. For frying, simmering, and boiling, use the same number of coals as the diameter of the Dutch oven at the bottom only, with lid on or off.

- For baking, the usual target temperature is 350°F. There are a few ways to achieve this:

   a. Determine the diameter of your Dutch oven, and double that number to determine the total number of coals to use. Two-thirds of the number would the number of coals to be placed on top and one-third would be the number of coals to go under the Dutch oven. So, for a 12-inch Dutch oven, double the number would be 24. Two-thirds of 24 would be 16 and one-third would be 8. So you are to put 16 coals on the lid and 8 underneath. Some put three-quarters of the

135

diameter on top and one-quarter underneath. The main thing is that there should be more coals on the lid than at the bottom.

b. Use the "Rule of 4". Add 4 to the diameter of your pot to get the number of coals for the lid, and subtract 4 for the number of coals to be put at the bottom. Some use the "Rule of 3," which follows the same formula except that 3 is added and subtracted instead of 4.

c. Use this simple table:

Diameter		No. of Coals Needed to Reach Desired Temperature					
		325°	350°	375°	400°	425°	450°
8"	Top	10	11	11	12	13	14
	Bottom	5	5	6	6	6	6
10"	Top	13	14	16	17	18	19
	Bottom	6	7	7	8	9	10
12"	Top	16	17	18	19	21	22
	Bottom	7	8	9	10	10	11
14"	Top	20	21	22	24	25	26
	Bottom	10	11	12	12	13	14

d. A simpler way is to simply multiply the diameter by two to get the number of coals needed. Simply arrange as many coals as will fit on the lid and place the rest at the bottom of the Dutch oven. Even without further computation, you will more or less arrive at the correct ratio.

- It's safer to use fewer coals than what is suggested, if you need to avoid burning and wasting food.

- Another great thing about Dutch ovens is that they can be stacked, saving space and fuel. In stacking, remember to put food that requires more heat (like stews) on top and those that require the least heat (like desserts) at the bottom.

- The initial layers of coal will last for about 1 hour. It's best to keep watch and add more coals as needed, especially when the dish requires more than an hour to cook.

- Just relax and enjoy the food, the cooking, and the outdoors. Remember, people in the past survived even without exact measurements!

Made in the USA
Middletown, DE
07 October 2023

40418006R00080